BLOOM
Founded by | arihant

Olympiad ACE

A Comprehensive Practice Book

for School Olympiads & Talent Search Exams

COMPUTER

Class 5

by

Sanjib Pal

Olympiad ACE

BLOOM

Bloom Cap Edu Ventures Pvt. Ltd.

卐 **Administrative & Production Office**

'Ramchhaya' 4577/15, Agarwal Road, Darya Ganj, New Delhi -110002
Tele: 011- 47630600, 43518550

卐 **PRICE** ₹125.00

Published by Arihant Publications (I) Ltd.

For further information about the books log on to
www.bloomcap.org

Follow us on

Preface

"Future belongs to those Who prepares for it today"

School Olympiads are National & International level competitions conducted by different Government, Non-Government & Educational Organisations with the purpose of making the children ready to face competitive exams.

The challenging Questions asked in Olympiads motivate them to learn more & more and bring out the best result with improved academic performance. The Awards & Scholarship offered by Olympiads motivate children to aspire & strive for doing better and emerge out to be the best.

Science Olympiads

Being a Scientist or Engineer or Doctor has always been a dream of each school going child. A good command over Science is a must for any of these. Questions of Science Olympiads are structured to help students to develop scientific temperament & motivate them to understand the concepts of science. They also focuses on improving existing knowledge of a student by adding more information.

'Bloom Science Olympiad Study Book Class 5' is a perfect resource to Study & Practice for Olympiad Exams and other National & State Level Talent Search Exams & Other Competitions.

Some Special Features of Bloom Science Olympiad Study Books are;

- Chapterwise Exercises having different types of Objective Questions; Analytical, Applications, Remembering etc, at par with the Olympiad Level.
- Detailed Explanation for each question.
- Olympiad Pattern Practice Sets at the end.

This book is prepared by Expert Panel with the utmost care, still if you have any suggestions regarding its improvement then feel free to contact us at support@bloomcap.org. We will try to inculcate your suggestions in the further editions.

Contents

01

Fundamentals of Computer

MCQs 1 Mark Questions

1. In which memory is the page stored, when we visit a web page on internet?
(a) RAM
(b) Cache
(c) Auxiliary
(d) None of these

2. It contains a basic set of instructions.
(a) BIOS
(b) RAM
(c) ROM
(d) Cache

3. The speed at which computer can perform calculations is
(a) one instruction per second
(b) hundred instructions per second
(c) million instructions per second
(d) twenty thousand instructions per second

4. In making movies, computers are used for adding
(a) special effects
(b) prints
(c) games
(d) magic

5. Computers are used for controlling the functions of .... in Space Technology.
(a) planets
(b) satellites
(c) special effects
(d) animations

6. The technology used by second generation computers is
(a) Transistors
(b) Integrated Circuit (IC)
(c) Both (a) and (b)
(d) None of these

7. The technology that creates characters by means of reflected light and is commonly used in digital watches and laptop computers is called
(a) LED (b) LCD
(c) EGA (d) None of these

8. In 1984, who introduced the first desktop laser printer, called the LaserJet?
(a) Hewlett-Packard (b) IBM
(c) Canon (d) Apple

9. CD-RW stands for
(a) Compact disc Re-writable (b) Compact disc - Read and write
(c) Compact data - Recordable (d) Compact data - Reader

10. Which of the following is not a portable device?
(a) 
(b) 
(c) 

(d) 

11. Which of the following computer languages is used for Artificial Intelligence?
(a) FORTRAN (b) C
(c) PROLOG (d) None of these

12. The calculations and data comparison such as "If X|Y then Z = X + Y" performed by CPU is called as
(a) data (b) output
(c) processing (d) Input

13. A general purpose single-user microcomputer designed to be operated by one person at a time is called?
(a) Special – purpose computer (b) KIPS
(c) PC (d) None of these

14. The invisible concentric circles on the platters are called
(a) rings (b) spots
(c) tracks (d) lines

15. Which software is used to create full motion video, animation, sound, etc.?
(a) Utility (b) Multimedia
(c) Accounting (d) Word processing

16. Which device can understand the difference between data and programs?
(a) Input device (b) Output device
(c) Memory (d) Microprocessor

17. In analog computer,
(a) input is first converted to digital form. (b) input is never converted to digital form.
(c) output is displayed in digital form. (d) All of these

18. In latest Generation computers, instructions are executed
(a) parallel only (b) sequentially only
(c) Both sequentially and parall (d) All of these

19. Distributed operating systems were used in which generation of Computers?
(a) First (b) Third (c) Second (d) fourth

20. Which of the following is High Level Language?
(a) ADA (b) COBOL
(c) FORTRAN (d) All of these

21. A light pen is
(a) mechanical input device (b) optical input device
(c) electrical input device (d) optical output device

22. Daisy wheel printer is also known as
(a) Golf Ball printer (b) Line Printer
(c) Laser Printer (d) Dotted wheel Printer

MCQs 2 Marks Questions

23. Match the following lists.

	List I		List II
A.	All modern computer operates on	1.	Cache memory
B.	This has shortest access time	2.	Data
C.	Memory which can be read only	3.	Magnetic core
D.	First generation computer use this as primary memory	4.	ROM

Codes

	A	B	C	D		A	B	C	D
(a)	2	1	4	3	(b)	4	3	1	2
(c)	1	2	3	4	(d)	3	1	4	2

24. Which statements is/are correct?

I. PHP stands for Hypertext preprocessor.

II. CUI can be operated with mouse and keyboard both.

Codes

(a) Only I (b) Only II

(c) Both I and II (d) Neither I nor II

25. Which of the following statements is/are true?

I. A computer is a versatile machine which calculates at high speed.

II. A computer is not at all a reliable machine.

Codes

(a) Only I (b) Only II

(c) Both I and II (d) Neither I nor II

26. Which of the following match is incorrect?

List I	List II
I. He designed the first general purpose electronic digital computer 'ENIAC'	Von-Neumann
II. It was the first stored program in electronic computer which was built in 1949 at Cambridge University in England	EDSAC
III. A storage device which is used to store data & information external to the main storage is known as	Backing storage

Codes

(a) Only I (b) Only III

(c) I and II (d) II and III

Darken your choice with HB Pencil

1. ⓐ ⓑ ⓒ ⓓ	6. ⓐ ⓑ ⓒ ⓓ	11. ⓐ ⓑ ⓒ ⓓ	16. ⓐ ⓑ ⓒ ⓓ	21. ⓐ ⓑ ⓒ ⓓ	26. ⓐ ⓑ ⓒ ⓓ
2. ⓐ ⓑ ⓒ ⓓ	7. ⓐ ⓑ ⓒ ⓓ	12. ⓐ ⓑ ⓒ ⓓ	17. ⓐ ⓑ ⓒ ⓓ	22. ⓐ ⓑ ⓒ ⓓ	
3. ⓐ ⓑ ⓒ ⓓ	8. ⓐ ⓑ ⓒ ⓓ	13. ⓐ ⓑ ⓒ ⓓ	18. ⓐ ⓑ ⓒ ⓓ	23. ⓐ ⓑ ⓒ ⓓ	
4. ⓐ ⓑ ⓒ ⓓ	9. ⓐ ⓑ ⓒ ⓓ	14. ⓐ ⓑ ⓒ ⓓ	19. ⓐ ⓑ ⓒ ⓓ	24. ⓐ ⓑ ⓒ ⓓ	
5. ⓐ ⓑ ⓒ ⓓ	10. ⓐ ⓑ ⓒ ⓓ	15. ⓐ ⓑ ⓒ ⓓ	20. ⓐ ⓑ ⓒ ⓓ	25. ⓐ ⓑ ⓒ ⓓ	

02

Hardware and Software

MCQs 1 Mark Questions

1. The part of primary memory which consists of important information necessary to execute user and application programs is
(a) RAM (b) Hard disk (c) ROM (d) Both (a) and (c)

2. In .... storage device, the access time is effectively independent of the location of data.
(a) Direct access (b) Secondary storage
(c) Primary storage (d) Indirect access

3. The measurement unit of quality of printers is DPI. What does DPI stands for?
(a) Data Per Inch (b) Dots Per Inch
(c) Data Processing Implementation (d) None of these

4. 1 GB = ...
(a) 1 Billion Bytes (b) 1024 KB
(c) 1 Trillion Bytes (d) 1 Thousand Bytes

5. One of the earliest operating system was
(a) DOS (b) MAC
(c) Windows (d) Both (a) and (b)

6. This is the first program loaded into the computer and remains in the memory all times.
(a) MS Word (b) Internet Explorer
(c) Operating System (d) MS DOS

7. The process of turning on the system and loading operating system in the primary memory is known as

(a) booting (b) loading
(c) downloading (d) processing

8. Programs designed to perform specific task are known as

(a) System Software (b) Application Software
(c) Utility Programs (d) Operating System

9. A small amount of memory included in the processor for high speed access is called

(a) register (b) cache
(c) RAM (d) ROM

10. Secondary storage device is needed to

(a) perform arithmetic and logical calculations.
(b) store small value of data.
(c) print output results.
(d) store large volumes of data and programs that exceed the capacity of the main memory.

11. A correct fact on dot matrix printers is that

(a) they tend do have higher quality that ink jet printers.
(b) it is very expensive.
(c) it is noisy in operation and cannot produce the high quality printing.
(d) it can be used as fax machine.

12. Which device of computer operation dispenses with the use of the keyboard?

(a) Joystick (b) Mouse
(c) Light pen (d) Scanner

13. The section of the CPU that selects, interpret and sees to the execution of program instructions is

(a) Control unit (b) Register unit
(c) ALU (d) memory

14. An optical input device that interprets pencil marks on paper media is called?

(a) MICR (b) OMR
(c) OCR (d) Barcode reader

15. Codes consisting of light and dark marks which may be optically read is known as

(a) Mnemonics (b) Barcode
(c) Decoder (d) All of these

16. Identify the device shown here and select the statement which is correct about it.

(a) It is a small drive that connects to a computer directly through a USB port with a low storage capacity.
(b) It is a storage medium with a greater audiovisual data storage capacity.
(c) This primary storage device is directly attached to the motherboard's disk controller.
(d) It spins around and can store information when placed in the disk reader.

MCQs 2 Marks Questions

17. Which of the following statements is/are correct?

I. In secondary memory, the program and data is located before ALU and Control Unit of a computer.
II. In internal memory, the program and data is located before ALU and Control Unit of a computer.
III. In hard disk, the program and data is located before ALU and Control Unit of a computer.

Codes

(a) I and II
(b) Only II
(c) Only III
(d) All of these

18. Which of the following statements holds true about process of booting?

I. Power on computer → Power On Self Test (POST) is completed → OS is loaded → System configuration is completed → System utilities are loaded → User is authenticated.
II. Power on computer → OS is loaded → Power On Self Test (POST) is completed → System configuration is completed → System utilities are loaded → User is authenticated.

Codes

(a) Only I
(b) Only II
(c) Both I and II
(d) Neither I nor II

19. Unscramble the given letters and select the option with which it relates.

FTASRWEO

(a) It is a set of instructions, data or programs used to operate computers and execute specific tasks.

(b) It is directed by the software to execute any command or instruction .

(c) It can hold and store information both temporarily and permanently.

(d) It allows the user to enter information into the system, or control its operation.

20. Select the incorrect statement.

(a) The process of dividing the disk into tracks and sectors is called Formatting.

(b) The main directory of a disk is called Folder.

(c) To enable the computer to read the disk, it is inserted in Disk Drive.

(d) All of the above

21. Which of the following statement holds true about ROM?

I. ROM is non-volatile memory.

II. ROM contains information required to run application programs.

Codes

(a) Only I (b) Only II

(c) Both I and II (d) Neither I nor II

22. Match the following lists.

List I	**List II**
A. Supervisor of computer activity.	1. Antivirus
B. An multi user operating system.	2. Process Management
C. It takes care of creation and deletion of process.	3. UNIX
D. It is a utility software.	4. Control Unit

Codes

	A	B	C	D		A	B	C	D
(a)	4	3	2	1	(b)	2	4	3	1
(c)	2	1	4	3	(d)	1	3	2	4

Darken your choice with HB Pencil

1.	ⓐ ⓑ ⓒ ⓓ	5.	ⓐ ⓑ ⓒ ⓓ	9.	ⓐ ⓑ ⓒ ⓓ	13.	ⓐ ⓑ ⓒ ⓓ	17.	ⓐ ⓑ ⓒ ⓓ	21.	ⓐ ⓑ ⓒ ⓓ
2.	ⓐ ⓑ ⓒ ⓓ	6.	ⓐ ⓑ ⓒ ⓓ	10.	ⓐ ⓑ ⓒ ⓓ	14.	ⓐ ⓑ ⓒ ⓓ	18.	ⓐ ⓑ ⓒ ⓓ	22.	ⓐ ⓑ ⓒ ⓓ
3.	ⓐ ⓑ ⓒ ⓓ	7.	ⓐ ⓑ ⓒ ⓓ	11.	ⓐ ⓑ ⓒ ⓓ	15.	ⓐ ⓑ ⓒ ⓓ	19.	ⓐ ⓑ ⓒ ⓓ		
4.	ⓐ ⓑ ⓒ ⓓ	8.	ⓐ ⓑ ⓒ ⓓ	12.	ⓐ ⓑ ⓒ ⓓ	16.	ⓐ ⓑ ⓒ ⓓ	20.	ⓐ ⓑ ⓒ ⓓ		

03

Introduction to Multimedia

MCQs 1 Mark Questions

1. Which image files are lossy format ?

(a) GIF (b) MPEG
(c) JPEG (d) PNG

2. Which file creates a perfect reproduction of the original images ?

(a) GIF (b) Nx View
(c) Shockwave (d) JPG

3. Images included in many software t..les are called

(a) Popups (b) Clipart
(c) .jpg files (d) .tiff files

4. Which of the following is a technique to blend two or more images to form a new image?

(a) Modeling (b) Wraping
(c) Animating (d) Morphing

5. Moving Picture Experts Group (MPEG) is used to compress

(a) frames (b) images
(c) audio (d) video

6. MIDI stand for

(a) Musical Instrument Digital Interface (b) Musical Instrument Digital Instruction
(c) Musical Instrument Design Interface (d) Multimedia Instrument Digital Interface

7. The sequence of frames is called

(a) image (b) animation
(c) video (d) None of these

8. Which of the following is the only lossless format that Web Browser supports?
(a) PNG (b) JPEG
(c) TIFF (d) BMP

9. What is the most common way to discover a media type?
(a) By file name (b) By file extension
(c) By file location (d) None of these

10. What is the extension of videos stored in Real Video format?
(a) .rm (b) .wm
(c) Both (a) and (b) (d) None of these

11. Is MIDI format editable?
(a) True (b) False
(c) Can't say (d) None of these

12. Most lossy format in audio offers a range of degree of compression. The degree is measured in
(a) bit rate (b) frequency of data
(c) data rate (d) size of file

13. Online Radio station uses which format to deliver continuous flow of data?
(a) .wmv (b) .mpeg
(c) .mp3 (d) None of these

14. The number of pixels present in an image per unit area is called
(a) frames (b) resolution (c) dots (d) image

15. Which was the first 3D movie in Indian cinema?
(a) Chhota Bheem (b) My Friend Ganesha
(c) Ramayan (d) My Dear Kutti Chathan

16. The following icon belongs to which media player?

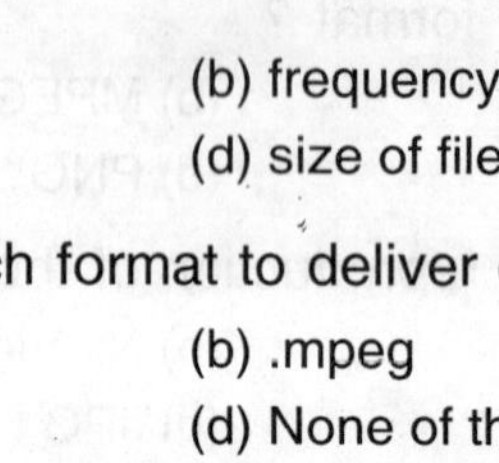

(a) Windows media player (b) VLC
(c) Both (a) and (b) (d) None of these

17. .... is a computer graphic technique that allows artist to create realistic effects like destruction, fire, smoke, particles in air etc. in their scenes.

(a) 3D Rendering (b) 3D Simulation
(c) 3D Merging (d) None of these

18. A Flight Simulator is an example of which media type?

(a) Interactive media (b) Integrated media
(c) Passive media (d) None of these

MCQs 2 Marks Questions

19. Select the incorrect match.

(a) .mid files – instrumental files.
(b) .wav files – not supported in browsers.
(c) .mp3 files – needs an application to be installed.
(d) .wma files – are lossless compression.

20. Which of the following statements holds true about multimedia?

I. It is an interactive media and provides multiple ways to represent information to the user.
II. It provides an interaction between users and digital information.

Codes

(a) Only I (b) Only II
(c) Both I and II (d) Neither I nor II

Darken your choice with HB Pencil

1.	ⓐ ⓑ ⓒ ⓓ	5.	ⓐ ⓑ ⓒ ⓓ	9.	ⓐ ⓑ ⓒ ⓓ	13.	ⓐ ⓑ ⓒ ⓓ	17.	ⓐ ⓑ ⓒ ⓓ
2.	ⓐ ⓑ ⓒ ⓓ	6.	ⓐ ⓑ ⓒ ⓓ	10.	ⓐ ⓑ ⓒ ⓓ	14.	ⓐ ⓑ ⓒ ⓓ	18.	ⓐ ⓑ ⓒ ⓓ
3.	ⓐ ⓑ ⓒ ⓓ	7.	ⓐ ⓑ ⓒ ⓓ	11.	ⓐ ⓑ ⓒ ⓓ	15.	ⓐ ⓑ ⓒ ⓓ	19.	ⓐ ⓑ ⓒ ⓓ
4.	ⓐ ⓑ ⓒ ⓓ	8.	ⓐ ⓑ ⓒ ⓓ	12.	ⓐ ⓑ ⓒ ⓓ	16.	ⓐ ⓑ ⓒ ⓓ	20.	ⓐ ⓑ ⓒ ⓓ

04

MS Paint 2016

MCQs 1 Mark Questions

1. Which of the following is not a valid option to rotate an image?
   (a) Rotate left 90°
   (b) Rotate left 180°
   (c) Flip Vertical
   (d) Flip horizontal

2. In View Tab of MS Paint, which of the following options we will find?
   (a) Zoom In
   (b) Zoom Out
   (c) 100%
   (d) All of these

3. MS Paint program can be in which mode?
   (a) Color Mode
   (b) Black and White Mode
   (c) Both (a) and (b)
   (d) Grayscale Mode

4. Which tool is the default extension of MS Paint file?
   (a) .BMP
   (b) .JPEG
   (C) .TIFF
   (d) None of these

5. Which will you use to fill the entire picture or an enclosed shape with color?
   (a) Airbrush
   (b) Fill with color
   (c) Pencil
   (d) Color box

6. To select any square or rectangular part of the picture, which toolbox will you use?
   (a) Line
   (b) Fill with color
   (c) Free-form select
   (d) Select

7. What is the default background color in MS Paint?
   (a) Yellow
   (b) Aqua
   (c) Blue
   (d) White

8. Which of the following group is not available in the Home tab of Ribbon Bar?

(a) Clipboard (b) Image

(c) Tool (d) View

9. MS Paint application is available in which of the following operating system ?

(a) Linux (b) Windows

(c) DOS (d) MAC OS

10. Which shape cannot be drawn with the use of line tool?

(a) 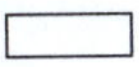 (b) 

(c) 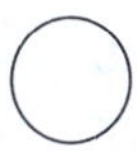 (d) 

11. Which of the following indicates the current foreground and background colors?

(a) Free-Form (b) Eraser

(c) Color box (d) Select

12. Which option should we select to change the height and width of an image in centimetres?

(a) Home tab of Ribbon (b) Properties option under file tab

(c) Design tab Ribbon (d) View tab of Ribbon

13. ....is the default foreground color in MS Paint.

(a) Black (b) White

(c) Green (d) Brown

14. Which key combination is used to decrease the size of shape, brush, line?

(a) Ctrl + - (b) Ctrl + +

(c)Alt + X (d) Ctrl + U

15. This part of MS Paint window is called

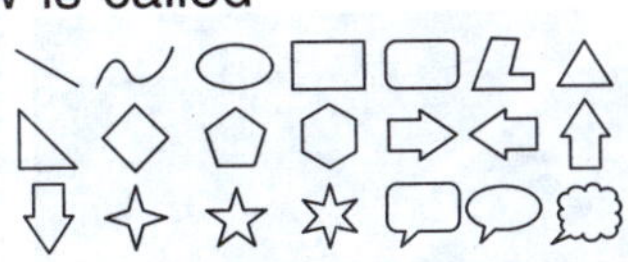

(a) tool panel (b) ribbon

(c) shapes (d) brushes

16. You can also cut and resize the image by using .... tool.

(a) Cut (b) Resize

(c) Crop (d) Both (b) and (c)

17. To invert a picture or drawing at the same place, we use

(a) Flip/ Rotate (b) Invert
(c) Edit (d) Resize

18. To show or hide Status Bar in which tab we can see the option?

(a) View Tab (b) Home Tab
(c) File Tab (d) None of these

19. .... are used to align the object in an image.

(a) Gridlines (b) Ruler
(c) Thumbnail (d) None of these

20. Properties option will give the details about the current image such as

(a) last saved (b) size on disk
(c) resolution (d) All of these

21. Using the size option what changes can be done to the image?

(a) To increase/decrease the line thickness of the Border of the image.
(b) To resize the image.
(c) To decrease/increase the size of the image.
(d) None of the above

MCQs 2 Marks Questions

Direction (22-24) Look at the given image of MS Paint window and answer the questions that follows.

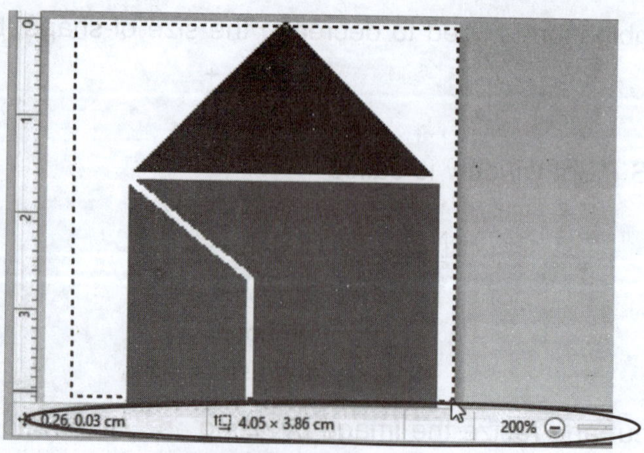

22. The circled portion of image is of
   (a) status bar
   (b) access bar
   (c) quick access toolbar
   (d) title bar

23. What is 4.05 x 3.86 cm shown in image?
   (a) Dimensions of the drawing area
   (b) Dimensions of the rectangular selection of drawing
   (c) Dimensions of the selected area of a drawing
   (d) Dimensions of the transparent selection

24. What is 0.26, 0.03 cm shown in image?
   (a) Cursor position
   (b) Dimensions of the drawing area
   (c) Dimensions of the selected area of a drawing
   (d) None of the above

25. By selecting, which type of brush we can make this type of painting?

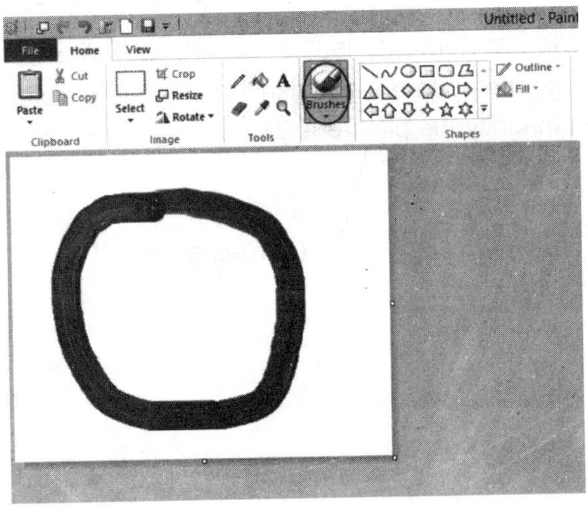

   (a) Oil Brush
   (b) Crayon
   (c) Marker
   (d) Calligraphy Brush

26. Match the following lists.

	List I		List II
A.	Fill a section with color	1.	
B.	Color with an airbrush	2.	
C.	Pick a color	3.	
D.	Color with a brush	4.	

Codes

	A	B	C	D		A	B	C	D
(a)	4	3	2	1	(b)	1	2	3	4
(c)	2	3	1	4	(d)	3	4	2	1

27. Which of the following statements is/are true about Magnifier Tool?

I. It is used to enlarge the apparent size like zoom in the picture.

II. Maximum size to magnify the picture is 2X.

Codes

(a) Only I

(b) Only II

(c) Both I and II

(d) Neither I nor II

Darken your choice with HB Pencil

1.	ⓐ ⓑ ⓒ ⓓ	6.	ⓐ ⓑ ⓒ ⓓ	11.	ⓐ ⓑ ⓒ ⓓ	16.	ⓐ ⓑ ⓒ ⓓ	21.	ⓐ ⓑ ⓒ ⓓ	26.	ⓐ ⓑ ⓒ ⓓ
2.	ⓐ ⓑ ⓒ ⓓ	7.	ⓐ ⓑ ⓒ ⓓ	12.	ⓐ ⓑ ⓒ ⓓ	17.	ⓐ ⓑ ⓒ ⓓ	22.	ⓐ ⓑ ⓒ ⓓ	27.	ⓐ ⓑ ⓒ ⓓ
3.	ⓐ ⓑ ⓒ ⓓ	8.	ⓐ ⓑ ⓒ ⓓ	13.	ⓐ ⓑ ⓒ ⓓ	18.	ⓐ ⓑ ⓒ ⓓ	23.	ⓐ ⓑ ⓒ ⓓ		
4.	ⓐ ⓑ ⓒ ⓓ	9.	ⓐ ⓑ ⓒ ⓓ	14.	ⓐ ⓑ ⓒ ⓓ	19.	ⓐ ⓑ ⓒ ⓓ	24.	ⓐ ⓑ ⓒ ⓓ		
5.	ⓐ ⓑ ⓒ ⓓ	10.	ⓐ ⓑ ⓒ ⓓ	15.	ⓐ ⓑ ⓒ ⓓ	20.	ⓐ ⓑ ⓒ ⓓ	25.	ⓐ ⓑ ⓒ ⓓ		

05

MS Word 2016

MCQs 1 Mark Questions

1. Choose the correct sequence of steps to open MS Word.
(a) Start–All programs–MS Office–MS Word
(b) Start–program–accessories–MS Office
(c) Start–program–accessories–MS Word
(d) Start–program–documents–MS Word

2. Which of the following effect cannot be applied on a text ?
(a) Superscript (b) Bold (c) Hidden (d) Subscript

3. $\underline{AB^2}$ is example of
(a) superscript (b) subscript
(c) underline (d) Both (a) and (c)

4. Which shortcut key in MS Word is used for jumping the cursor to starting position of a document?
(a) CTRL+HOME (b) CTRL+END
(c) CTRL+TAB (d) CTRL+DEL

5. The process of changing the appearance of selected text in MS Word document is called
(a) Booting (b) Formatting
(c) Designing (d) Aligning

6. In MS Word, by default documents print in which mode?
(a) Portrait (b) Landscape
(c) Print view (d) None of these

7. What is the default text alignment of MS Word document?
(a) Left (b) Right (c) Center (d) Justify

8. Select the steps to make a text hyperlinked.
(a) Page layout->proofing
(b) Insert->links->hyperlink
(c) Insert->add link->hyperlink
(d) Home->editing

9. Which tab of ribbon should you use to insert symbol like @ in MS Word document?
(a) Home
(b) Design
(c) Page layout
(d) Insert

10. .... key is used to check the spellings and grammar mistakes in MS Word.
(a) F7
(b) Alt+F4
(c) Alt+F7
(d) F12

11. The green line means .... under a sentence in a paragraph.
(a) spelling mistake
(b) grammatical error
(c) synonyms
(d) spacing error

12. .... option is used to view the document as it will appear on the printed page.
(a) Bookmarks
(b) Print Preview
(c) View
(d) Print

13. WordArt feature is found in which group of MS word?
(a) Text group
(b) Illustration
(c) Font group
(d) Link group

14. The feature of MS Word that provides list of synonyms is
(a) Find command
(b) Thesaurus
(c) Replace command
(d) Synonyms

15. .... is a preloaded group of images and pictures that can be imported into a document.
(a) Clipart
(b) Shapes
(c) Watermark
(d) Template

16. Which is the shortcut key used for changing font style, font color and font size?
(a) CTRL + D
(b) CTRL + B
(c) CTRL + E
(d) CTRL + T

17. Drop cap feature is available in .... tab of MS Word.
(a) Insert
(b) Design
(c) Home
(d) Review

18. ....feature of MS word is used to send the same letter to different address.

(a) Template (b) Email merge

(c) Mail merge (d) None of these

19. Which of the following icon can be used to copy and paste the formatting of existing paragraph ?

(a)  (b) 

(c) Aa (d) 

20.  Icon is used in MS word for?

(a) Fill color (b) Background

(c) Shading (d) Highlight

21. Which of the following is default viewing mode of MS Word?

(a)  (b) 

(c)  (d) 

22. Choose the incorrect statements about header and footer in MS Word.

(a) You can specify a unique header and footer for the first page of the document.

(b) You cannot apply drop cap feature in header and footer.

(c) You cannot insert an image in header and footer area.

(d) Both (a) and (b) are incorrect

23. Choose the correct statement about gutter margin.

(a) Gutter margin is added to the right margin when printing.

(b) Gutter margin is added to the binding side of the page when printing.

(c) Gutter margin is added to the left margin when printing.

(d) Gutter margin is added to the outside of the page when printing.

MCQs 2 Marks Questions

24. Match the following lists.

List I	List II
A. 	1. top border
B. 	2. bottom border
C. 	3. left border
D. 	4. right border

Codes

	A	B	C	D
(a)	4	3	1	2
(b)	2	3	1	4
(c)	3	4	2	1
(d)	4	3	2	1

25. Which of the following is/are function of MS Word?

I. Creating, editing, saving documents.
II. Protecting the documents with passwords.
III. Correcting spelling and grammatical errors.

Codes

(a) I and II
(b) II and III
(c) I, II and III
(d) Only II

Darken your choice with HB Pencil

1. ⓐ ⓑ ⓒ ⓓ	6. ⓐ ⓑ ⓒ ⓓ	11. ⓐ ⓑ ⓒ ⓓ	16. ⓐ ⓑ ⓒ ⓓ	21. ⓐ ⓑ ⓒ ⓓ
2. ⓐ ⓑ ⓒ ⓓ	7. ⓐ ⓑ ⓒ ⓓ	12. ⓐ ⓑ ⓒ ⓓ	17. ⓐ ⓑ ⓒ ⓓ	22. ⓐ ⓑ ⓒ ⓓ
3. ⓐ ⓑ ⓒ ⓓ	8. ⓐ ⓑ ⓒ ⓓ	13. ⓐ ⓑ ⓒ ⓓ	18. ⓐ ⓑ ⓒ ⓓ	23. ⓐ ⓑ ⓒ ⓓ
4. ⓐ ⓑ ⓒ ⓓ	9. ⓐ ⓑ ⓒ ⓓ	14. ⓐ ⓑ ⓒ ⓓ	19. ⓐ ⓑ ⓒ ⓓ	24. ⓐ ⓑ ⓒ ⓓ
5. ⓐ ⓑ ⓒ ⓓ	10. ⓐ ⓑ ⓒ ⓓ	15. ⓐ ⓑ ⓒ ⓓ	20. ⓐ ⓑ ⓒ ⓓ	25. ⓐ ⓑ ⓒ ⓓ

06

MS Excel 2016

MCQs 1 Mark Questions

1. In MS Excel, the collection of worksheet is called
   (a) Excel sheet
   (b) Workbook
   (c) Table
   (d) Worksheet group
2. File created using MS Excel is by default save as
   (a) Document 1
   (b) Sheet 1
   (c) Book 1
   (d) Home
3. What is the smallest unit of Excel?
   (a) Sheet (b) Cell (c) Book (d) Document
4. An Excel workbook is a collection of
   (a) charts
   (b) files
   (c) spreadsheets
   (d) Both (a) and (c)
5. In MS Excel, which shortcut key is used to format cell?
   (a) CTRL+2 (b) CTRL+1 (c) CTRL+5 (d) CTRL+F
6. MS Excel files have default extension of
   (a) .xlw (b) .xlsx (c) .xlx (d) .wkl
7. In MS Excel, all formulas must begin with .... symbol.
   (a) @ (b) = (c) + (d) –
8. The default orientation of MS Excel worksheets is
   (a) portrait (b) landscape (c) horizontal (d) hanging
9. The basic function of MS Excel, used to join two or more text strings is
   (a) JOIN
   (b) CONCATENATE
   (c) VLOOKUP
   (d) SUMIF

10. Choose the correct shortcut key to enable filtering of selected cells in MS Excel.
(a) CTRL+ F
(b) CTRL+ SHIFT + L
(c) ALT + L
(d) SHIFT + F

11. A donut chart in Excel is similar to
(a) Pie chart
(b) Bubble chart
(c) Bar chart
(d) Scatter chart

12. .... feature is used to make headings visible even while scrolling in MS Excel.
(a) Freeze pane
(b) Fixed pane
(c) Freeze heading
(d) Paradox

13. .... is the address of first cell in Excel.
(a) A
(b) AA
(c) A1
(d) A:1

14. In Excel, ... function is used to adjust data of one or more cells into a single cell.
(a) text to text
(b) shrink to fit
(c) adjust text
(d) None of these

15. Choose the correct steps to open chart wizard in excel.
(a) View → Pictures → Chart
(b) View → Chart
(c) Insert → Pictures → Charts
(d) Insert → Chart

16. .... function is used to find biggest value in a range.
(a) CELLING
(b) DMAX
(c) LARGEST
(d) MAX

17. What is the output of given formula?
= LEN ("hello world")
(a) 10
(b) 11
(c) 15
(d) 13

18. Which of the following allows us to remove duplicate data from selected range of cells in MS Excel?
(a) 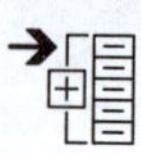
(b) 
(c) 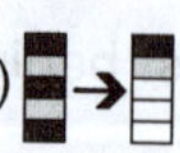
(d) 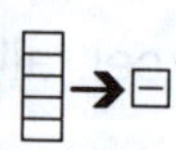

19.  Icon used for
(a) find data
(b) sorting
(c) what-if analysis
(d) data validation

MCQs 2 Marks Questions

20. Which one of the following options is correct about the given formula? Enter"=SUM (A1:A4)" in cell A5, it would

(a) Throw an error message because text values cannot be added.
(b) Display the average of all numbers.
(c) Display the correct sum of all numbers from A1 to A4.
(d) Display the sum of numbers of cell A1 and A4.

21. Find the incorrect statement about MS Excel.

(a) We can easily change the name of any worksheet in Excel.
(b) We cannot add both text and numbers in a worksheet.
(c) In Excel, by default numeric values are right aligned.
(d) In Excel, by default text data is left align.

22. Choose the correct statement(s) about auto sum function in MS Excel.

(a) Use to get the total count of rows.
(b) Use to get the total count of cells.
(c) Use to get the total count of columns.
(d) Use to get the total sum value of all the values in range of numeric cells.

23. Find the correct statement(s) about VLOOKUP function of MS Excel.

I. It looks up to the text in a cell.
II. Finds related records.

Codes

(a) Only I
(b) Only II
(c) Both I and II
(d) Neither I nor II

24. Match the following lists.

List I	List II
A. Returns the largest nearest integer.	1. COUNT()
B. Counts the total number of entries in the cells	2. CEILING()
C. Checks whether a condition is true or not	3. FLOOR()
D. Returns the smallest nearest integer	4. IF()

Codes

	A	B	C	D
(a)	2	4	3	1
(b)	2	1	4	3
(c)	1	4	3	2
(d)	2	4	1	3

25. Shown image belongs to which tab of MS Excel.

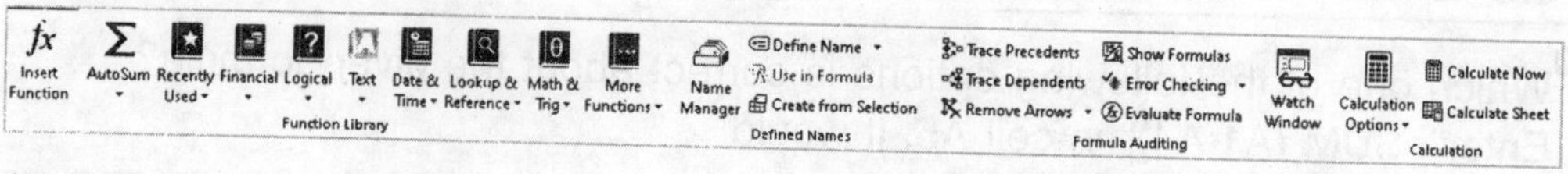

(a) Function (b) Data (c) Formulas (d) Review

26. Shown image created using which feature of MS Excel.

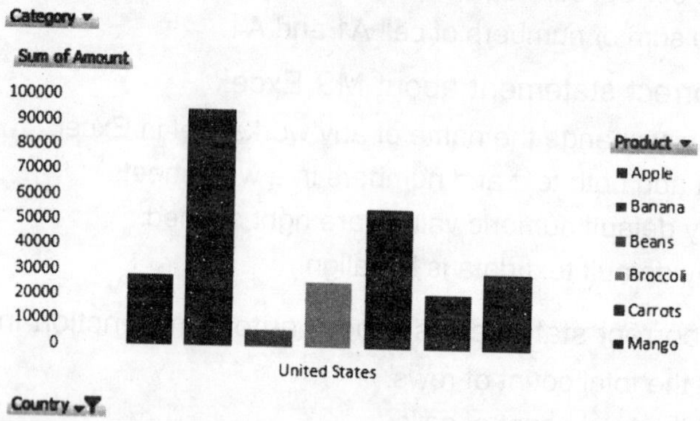

(a) Pie chart (b) Bar chart (c) Pivot chart (d) Pivot table

27. What type of conditional formatting is applied on the shown worksheet?

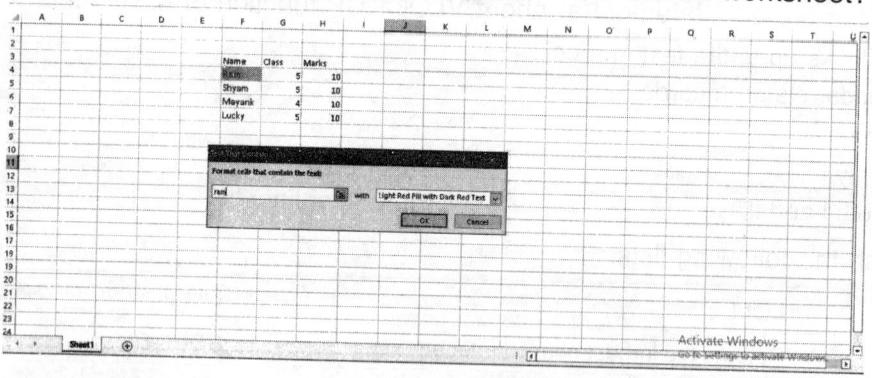

(a) Color scales (b) Data bars
(c) Highlight cells rules (d) None of these

Darken your choice with HB Pencil

1. (a) (b) (c) (d)	6. (a) (b) (c) (d)	11. (a) (b) (c) (d)	16. (a) (b) (c) (d)	21. (a) (b) (c) (d)	26. (a) (b) (c) (d)
2. (a) (b) (c) (d)	7. (a) (b) (c) (d)	12. (a) (b) (c) (d)	17. (a) (b) (c) (d)	22. (a) (b) (c) (d)	27. (a) (b) (c) (d)
3. (a) (b) (c) (d)	8. (a) (b) (c) (d)	13. (a) (b) (c) (d)	18. (a) (b) (c) (d)	23. (a) (b) (c) (d)	
4. (a) (b) (c) (d)	9. (a) (b) (c) (d)	14. (a) (b) (c) (d)	19. (a) (b) (c) (d)	24. (a) (b) (c) (d)	
5. (a) (b) (c) (d)	10. (a) (b) (c) (d)	15. (a) (b) (c) (d)	20. (a) (b) (c) (d)	25. (a) (b) (c) (d)	

07

MS PowerPoint 2016

MCQs 1 Mark Questions

1. Which one of the following MS PowerPoint view displays only the textual content?
(a) Outline view (b) Normal view (c) Slide Sorter view (d) Slide view

2. What is the direct command to open MS PowerPoint from the run dialog box?
(a) PPTX (b) PowerPoint (c) Powerpnt (d) Powerexe

3. Which shortcut key is used to duplicate selected slide in PowerPoint ?
(a) CTRL+M (b) CTRL+D
(c) CTRL+SHIFT+D (d) ALT+M

4. The objects which are used to hold the text in the slide are known as
(a) text box (b) placeholders
(c) text holders (d) Both B and C

5. To add a new slide in PowerPoint, which shortcut key is used ?
(a) CTRL+M (b) CTRL+N (c) CTRL+D (d) ALT+M

6. File that contains pre-made styles that can be used in presentation to create slides is called
(a) auto style (b) formatting (c) template (d) set up slideshow

7. The special effects used in slides in PowerPoint presentation are called
(a) animation (b) effects (c) transitions (d) slideshow

8. Which shortcut key is used for slideshow in PowerPoint?
(a) F5 (b) F9 (c) CTRL+F4 (d) ALT+F5

9. We use .... to add text in slides in PowerPoint presentation.
(a) text box (b) comment box
(c) text area (d) insert text

10. .... feature of PowerPoint gives you a miniature view of all slides.
    (a) Print preview (b) Slide view
    (c) Slide sorter view (d) Slideshow
11. Find, replace, select features are part of .... group.
    (a) Insert (b) Proofing
    (c) Format (d) Editing
12. .... is not a PowerPoint view.
    (a) Normal view (b) Print view
    (c) Notes Page view (d) Outline view
13. Choose the correct steps to add header and footer in handouts.
    (a) View->header and footer (b) View->handout master
    (c) View->page setup (d) View->handouts
14. .... shortcut key stops the slide show.
    (a) CTRL+S (b) CTRL+K
    (c) ESC Key (d) CTRL+Shift+C
15. Find the odd one out.
    (a) Appear (b) Fade (c) Translate (d) Wheel
16. Which is the shortcut key is used to open font dialog box in MS PowerPoint?
    (a) CTRL+Shift+O (b) CTRL+F4
    (c) CTRL+T (d) CTRL+Shift+F
17. What is the default orientation of MS PowerPoint slide ?
    (a) Portrait (b) Landscape (c) Vertical (d) None of these
18. .... feature helps us to create special text effects.
    (a) Text style (b) WordArt
    (c) Transition (d) Text decoration
19. Shape effect button on the format tab is use to apply
    (a) special effects in slide show (b) 3D rotation to a shape
    (c) text formatting (d) different shapes
20. Choose the correct icon of MS PowerPoint 2016.
    (a)  (b) 
    (c)  (d) 

21.  Icon is used for

(a) Preview animation
(b) Preview slideshow
(c) Preview transition
(d) None of these

MCQs 2 Marks Questions

22. Following image is belong to which group and tab of MS PowerPoint ?

(a) Animation group of animations tab.
(b) Set up group of transition tab.
(c) Set up group of slideshow tab.
(d) Set up slide show group of slide show tab.

23. Match the following lists.

	List I		List II
A.	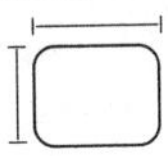	1.	Animation
B.	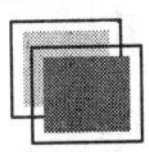 Fade	2.	Action
C.	 Fade	3.	Slide size
D.		4.	Transition

Codes

	A	B	C	D
(a)	3	4	1	2
(b)	1	3	2	4
(c)	2	1	4	3
(d)	2	3	4	1

24. Match the following lists.

	List I		List II
A.	Inserting new slide after currently selected slide	1.	CTRL+N
B.	Create a blank presentation	2.	CTRL+M
C.	Close the current open slide	3.	CTRL+W

Codes

	A	B	C		A	B	C
(a)	2	1	3	(b)	3	1	2
(c)	1	2	3	(d)	3	2	1

25. Choose the incorrect statement about MS PowerPoint.
(a) For inserting images into slides you can choose pictures from file using insert tab.
(b) You can type anything directly into a PowerPoint slide.
(c) Slide sorter view in PowerPoint gives you a miniature view of all slides.
(d) We can add different special effects in our presentation.

26. Which of the following statements is/are true about MS PowerPoint ?
I. We can use clipart features to add pictures in presentation.
II. In PowerPoint presentation slide can be modified only in slide sorter view.
III. In PowerPoint presentation normal view is the default presentation view.

Codes

(a) Only I (b) Only II
(c) I and II (d) I and III

27. Match the following lists.

	List I		List II
A.	Collection of sequentially arranged slides	1.	Themes
B.	Feature of PowerPoint that creates sample slide show	2.	Presentation
C.	Set of predesigned formats	3.	Text box
D.	Placeholder where you can enter your text	4.	Template

Codes

	A	B	C	D		A	B	C	D
(a)	2	4	1	3	(b)	2	1	4	3
(c)	2	3	1	4	(d)	3	2	4	1

Darken your choice with HB Pencil

1.	ⓐ ⓑ ⓒ ⓓ	6.	ⓐ ⓑ ⓒ ⓓ	11.	ⓐ ⓑ ⓒ ⓓ	16.	ⓐ ⓑ ⓒ ⓓ	21.	ⓐ ⓑ ⓒ ⓓ	26.	ⓐ ⓑ ⓒ ⓓ
2.	ⓐ ⓑ ⓒ ⓓ	7.	ⓐ ⓑ ⓒ ⓓ	12.	ⓐ ⓑ ⓒ ⓓ	17.	ⓐ ⓑ ⓒ ⓓ	22.	ⓐ ⓑ ⓒ ⓓ	27.	ⓐ ⓑ ⓒ ⓓ
3.	ⓐ ⓑ ⓒ ⓓ	8.	ⓐ ⓑ ⓒ ⓓ	13.	ⓐ ⓑ ⓒ ⓓ	18.	ⓐ ⓑ ⓒ ⓓ	23.	ⓐ ⓑ ⓒ ⓓ		
4.	ⓐ ⓑ ⓒ ⓓ	9.	ⓐ ⓑ ⓒ ⓓ	14.	ⓐ ⓑ ⓒ ⓓ	19.	ⓐ ⓑ ⓒ ⓓ	24.	ⓐ ⓑ ⓒ ⓓ		
5.	ⓐ ⓑ ⓒ ⓓ	10.	ⓐ ⓑ ⓒ ⓓ	15.	ⓐ ⓑ ⓒ ⓓ	20.	ⓐ ⓑ ⓒ ⓓ	25.	ⓐ ⓑ ⓒ ⓓ		

08

Windows 10

MCQs 1 Mark Questions

1. What is the default browser of Windows 10?
   (a) Internet explorer
   (b) Chrome browser
   (c) Microsoft edge
   (d) Firefox

2. Shortcut key for task switching in Windows 10.
   (a) ALT+TAB
   (b) ALT+S
   (c) CTRL+TAB
   (d) None of these

3. Which of the following is a text editor for Windows 10?
   (a) Notepad
   (b) WordPad
   (c) MS Word
   (d) All of these

4. Windows 10 is a
   (a) Programming language
   (b) System software
   (c) Operating system
   (d) Application software

5. Start button in Windows is used to
   (a) shutdown the system
   (b) run applications
   (c) device settings
   (d) All of these

6. A storage area for files and programs in Windows 10 is called
   (a) Desktop
   (b) Recycle bin
   (c) Folders
   (d) Safe box

7. Choose the correct steps to change screen resolution in Windows 10.
   (a) Display properties->projecting to this PC
   (b) Display properties->notification and actions
   (c) Start->settings->system->display->resolution
   (d) Display properties->tablet mode

8. .... is not an accessories program in Windows.

(a) VLC player (b) Notepad
(c) WordPad (d) Paint

9. Every deleted file or folder of the computer is stored in

(a) File Explorer (b) Recycle Bin
(c) This PC (d) None of these

10. .... is the shortcut key to paste a file /folder in Windows.

(a) CTRL+P (b) CTRL+A
(c) CTRL+V (d) CTRL+U

11. Shortcut key for virtual desktop in Windows 10.

(a) CTRL+ALT+N (b) CTRL+WINDOW LOGO KEY+D
(c) WINDOW LOGO KEY+D (d) ALT+TAB+D

12. System tray is located on

(a) status bar (b) task bar
(c) start menu (d) control panel

13. Feature of windows 10 that allows user to see notifications from different applications.

(a) System tray (b) Notification bar
(c) Action center (d) Task bar

14. Which of the following shortcut key can be used if you want to display your computer screen on another computer through Wi-Fi?

(a) Windows logo key +E (b) Windows logo key +B
(c) Windows logo key +P (d) Windows logo key +C

15. What is the view shown in the image is called in Windows 10?

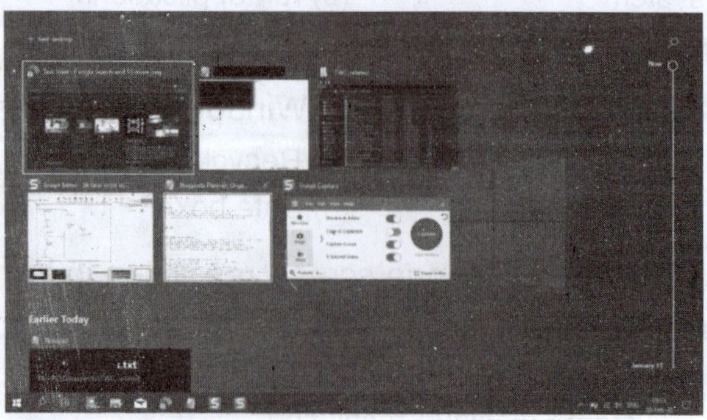

(a) Multitask view (b) Background view
(c) Task view (d) Quick look view

16. Area marked with arrow in the image is called

(a) status bar
(b) title bar
(c) task bar
(d) None of these

17. Shown image belongs to which component of Microsoft Windows.

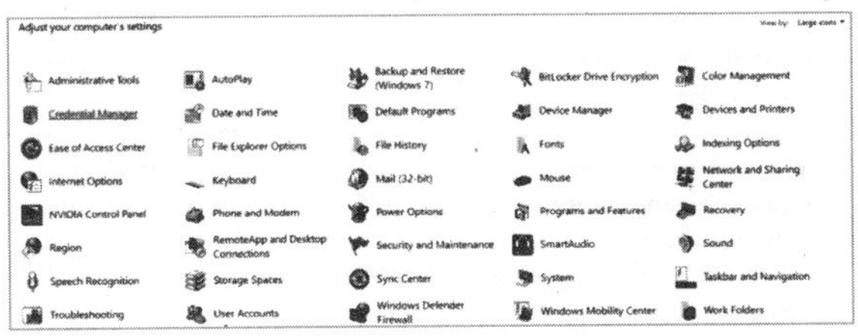

(a) Computer settings
(b) Administrative settings
(c) Control panel
(d) Network

18. Which of the following is not a version of Windows?

(a) Windows 10 pro
(b) Windows 10 education
(c) Windows IOT core
(d) Windows 10 business

MCQs 2 Marks Questions

19. Match the following lists.

	List I		List II
A.	Windows logo key+D	1.	lock the computer or switch accounts
B.	Windows logo key+TAB	2.	open the quick link menu
C.	Windows logo key+L	3.	show/hide desktop
D.	Windows logo key+X	4.	opens the task view

Codes

	A	B	C	D
(a)	4	3	1	2
(b)	3	4	1	2
(c)	3	1	2	4
(d)	2	3	4	1

20. Choose the incorrect statement about Windows 10.

(a) Windows 10 launched in year 2015.

(b) Windows 10 was successor of windows 8.1.

(c) Cortana was newly added feature in windows 10.

(d) Windows 10 don't have any mobile version.

21. What is the shortcut key to open the window shown in the image?

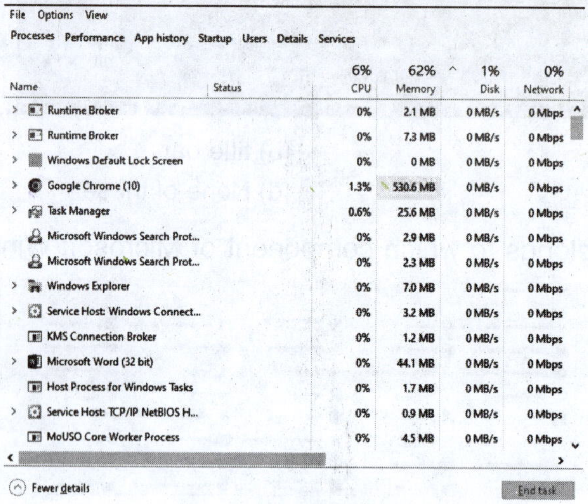

(a) CTRL+SHIFT+T (b) CTRL+SHIFT+TAB

(c) CTRL+SHIFT+ESC (d) CTRL+ALT+DEL

22. Choose the correct option to open registry editor in Windows.

(a) Right-click start button->select run->Type regedit->Enter.

(b) Right-click start button->select run->Type registryedit->Enter.

(c) Click Windows + R->type cmd click Enter->type regedit.

(d) Both (a) and (c)

23. Which of the following statements is/are incorrect about Windows 10?

(a) You can have multiple user account on a Windows computer.

(b) Microsoft edge is replaced by internet explorer in Windows 10.

(c) Windows 10 support 32 and 64 bit architecture.

(d) All are incorrect.

Darken your choice with HB Pencil

1.	ⓐ ⓑ ⓒ ⓓ	5.	ⓐ ⓑ ⓒ ⓓ	9.	ⓐ ⓑ ⓒ ⓓ	13.	ⓐ ⓑ ⓒ ⓓ	17.	ⓐ ⓑ ⓒ ⓓ	21.	ⓐ ⓑ ⓒ ⓓ
2.	ⓐ ⓑ ⓒ ⓓ	6.	ⓐ ⓑ ⓒ ⓓ	10.	ⓐ ⓑ ⓒ ⓓ	14.	ⓐ ⓑ ⓒ ⓓ	18.	ⓐ ⓑ ⓒ ⓓ	22.	ⓐ ⓑ ⓒ ⓓ
3.	ⓐ ⓑ ⓒ ⓓ	7.	ⓐ ⓑ ⓒ ⓓ	11.	ⓐ ⓑ ⓒ ⓓ	15.	ⓐ ⓑ ⓒ ⓓ	19.	ⓐ ⓑ ⓒ ⓓ	23.	ⓐ ⓑ ⓒ ⓓ
4.	ⓐ ⓑ ⓒ ⓓ	8.	ⓐ ⓑ ⓒ ⓓ	12.	ⓐ ⓑ ⓒ ⓓ	16.	ⓐ ⓑ ⓒ ⓓ	20.	ⓐ ⓑ ⓒ ⓓ		

09

Computer Networks

MCQs 1 Mark Questions

1. Which of the following is an advantage of computer networks?
(a) Easy resource sharing
(b) Improve readability and availability
(c) Enhance the performance
(d) All of the above

2. An example of PAN (Private Area Network) is
(a) Wi-Fi
(b) Bluetooth
(c) WLAN
(d) WIMAX

3. Which one of the following is a first computer network?
(a) MAC
(b) ARPANET
(c) ARPA
(d) NFS

4. Which of the following is not a network edge device?
(a) Server
(b) Smartphone
(c) PC
(d) Switch

5. What is true in context of hybrid client?
(a) Data processing and data storage done on a server.
(b) Data processing is done locally and server is used for storage.
(c) Data processing and storage done locally.
(d) None of the above

6. Suppose a device on a network wants to transmit data packets to all the devices in other network, what type of network casting we use for that?
(a) Multicast
(b) Broadcasting
(c) Limited broadcasting
(d) Direct broadcasting

7. A device that performs the encoding of digital signals into analog signals and vice versa is

(a) switch (b) gateway
(c) modem (d) web browser

8. What is the full form of Modem?

(a) Modulation demodulation (b) Modulator demodulator
(c) Modulator demodulation (d) Modulation demodulator

9. Set of rules that defines what data is communicated, how data is communicated and when data is communicated is known as

(a) message (b) protocols
(c) translator (d) server commands

10. A device that can forward packets across different networks that also uses different protocols is

(a) switch (b) NIC
(c) gateway (d) router

11. .... is a system that prevents from unauthorized access.

(a) Anti-virus (b) Malware
(c) Gateway (d) Firewall

12. .... is known as the most reliable network topology.

(a) Star topology (b) Bus topology
(c) Tree topology (d) Mesh topology

13. .... has minimum transmission speed.

(a) Twisted pair cable (b) Coaxial cable
(c) Fiber optical cable (d) Ribbon electric cables

14. .... is used to regenerate the weak signals.

(a) Repeater (b) Hub
(c) Switch (d) Gateway

15. FTP stands for

(a) File Translator Protocol (b) File Transfer Protocol
(c) File Transmission Protocol (d) File Transport Protocol

16. ....is a network topology in which all data passes through a central computer.

(a) Ring topology (b) Star topology
(c) Bus topology (d) Mesh topology

17. ....is a big computer that connects all the computers in a network.

(a) Host (b) Server

(c) Central CPU (d) Client

18. Which network architecture used in the given image?

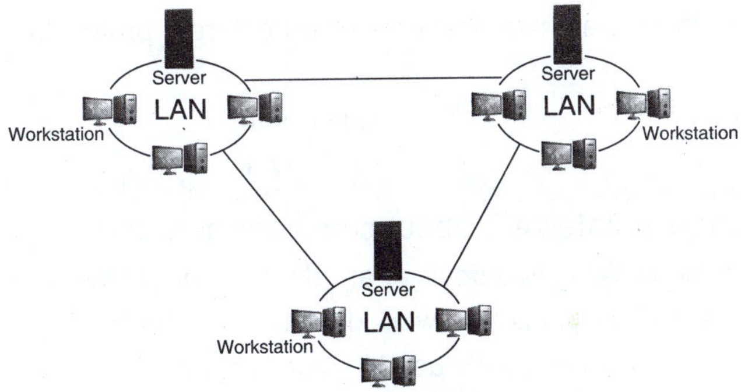

(a) MAN (b) MULTIPLE LAN

(c) WAN (d) PAN

19. Which topology is shown in the given image?

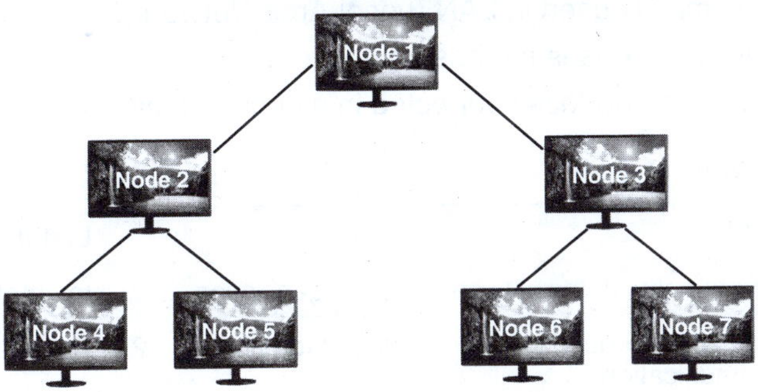

(a) Tree topology (b) Ring topology

(c) Hierarchical topology (d) Mesh topology

20. Select the odd one out.

(a) 

INC

(b) 

Repeater

(c) 

Gateway

(d) 

Server

MCQs 2 Marks Questions

21. Which of the following statements is/are correct about bridge?
    I. It is used to connect two LANs using similar protocols.
    II. It acts as an address filter.
    III. It can be used to connect two networks using different protocols.

    Codes
    (a) Only I
    (b) I and III
    (c) Both I and II
    (d) Only II

22. Choose the incorrect statement about computer networks.
    (a) In peer to peer networking two devices are directly connected with a dedicated link.
    (b) ARPANET is the first computer network developed in 1969.
    (c) Client server networking is mainly used in small network.
    (d) WAN is a largest network on the basis of geographical area.

23. Choose the incorrect statement about network topology.
    (a) Network topology is a geometric representation of a network.
    (b) Bus topology is mainly used in LAN (Local Area Network).
    (c) Network topology increases the cost of network.
    (d) In ring topology each node is connected in a circular loop.

24. Match the following lists.

	List I		List II
A.	Private network mainly used by an organization.	1.	Internet
B.	Used by an organization to provide external communication.	2.	Extranet
C.	Public network use to connect different networks.	3.	Intranet

Codes

	A	B	C
(a)	2	3	1
(b)	3	2	1
(c)	1	2	3
(d)	3	1	2

Darken your choice with HB Pencil

1.	ⓐ ⓑ ⓒ ⓓ	6.	ⓐ ⓑ ⓒ ⓓ	11.	ⓐ ⓑ ⓒ ⓓ	16.	ⓐ ⓑ ⓒ ⓓ	21.	ⓐ ⓑ ⓒ ⓓ
2.	ⓐ ⓑ ⓒ ⓓ	7.	ⓐ ⓑ ⓒ ⓓ	12.	ⓐ ⓑ ⓒ ⓓ	17.	ⓐ ⓑ ⓒ ⓓ	22.	ⓐ ⓑ ⓒ ⓓ
3.	ⓐ ⓑ ⓒ ⓓ	8.	ⓐ ⓑ ⓒ ⓓ	13.	ⓐ ⓑ ⓒ ⓓ	18.	ⓐ ⓑ ⓒ ⓓ	23.	ⓐ ⓑ ⓒ ⓓ
4.	ⓐ ⓑ ⓒ ⓓ	9.	ⓐ ⓑ ⓒ ⓓ	14.	ⓐ ⓑ ⓒ ⓓ	19.	ⓐ ⓑ ⓒ ⓓ	24.	ⓐ ⓑ ⓒ ⓓ
5.	ⓐ ⓑ ⓒ ⓓ	10.	ⓐ ⓑ ⓒ ⓓ	15.	ⓐ ⓑ ⓒ ⓓ	20.	ⓐ ⓑ ⓒ ⓓ		

10

Introduction to Scratch

MCQs 1 Mark Questions

1. Which of the following cannot be created using scratch?
   (a) Stories (b) Games
   (c) System software (d) Animations
2. When was scratch developed?
   (a) 2002 (b) 2009 (c) 2007 (d) None of these
3. What is stage in scratch programming?
   (a) Where characters are stored. (b) Background of your project.
   (c) Steps in the project. (d) Space where you present your project.
4. The duck in your jumping duck game in scratch is
   (a) stage (b) sprite
   (c) object (d) scratch image
5. What is the blue sky image shown behind your duck in jumping duck game in scratch is called?
   (a) Stage background (b) Sprite
   (c) Backdrop (d) Scratch image
6. From where, you can use different script blocks in your project.
   (a) Block palette (b) Scripts
   (c) Block area (d) None of these
7. How many built in blocks are there in scratch?
   (a) 6 (b) 10 (c) 9 (d) None of these
8. The place where you drag and drop command (code) blocks in scratch is called
   (a) block scripts (b) stage
   (c) block area (d) script area

9. Which script block, we can use if we want our character to say hello?
(a) Motion (b) Looks (c) Speech (d) Events

10. How can we create custom block in scratch?
(a) Using create block (b) Using my blocks
(c) Using add blocks (d) None of these

11. If we want some certain statements to repeat until we stops the program, we can use .... block.
(a) if/then (b) repeat (c) forever (d) repeat until

12. We can use .... script block if we want our sprite to move 10 steps.
(a) event (b) motion (c) sensing (d) move

13. We can delete a sprite from
(a) stage (b) sprites pane
(c) sprites menu (d) backdrop panel

14. .... allows the user to load random sprite or backdrop.
(a) Add random sprite (b) Random button
(c) Load button (d) Surprise button

15. Collection of command blocks that are interlock with each other to perform a certain task is called
(a) script (b) task panel
(c) command group (d) block group

16. Which of the following can be used to add backdrops in scratch?

(a)  (b)  (c)  (d) 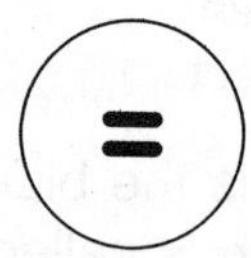

17. What will sprite do when you press the space key and left arrow key together?

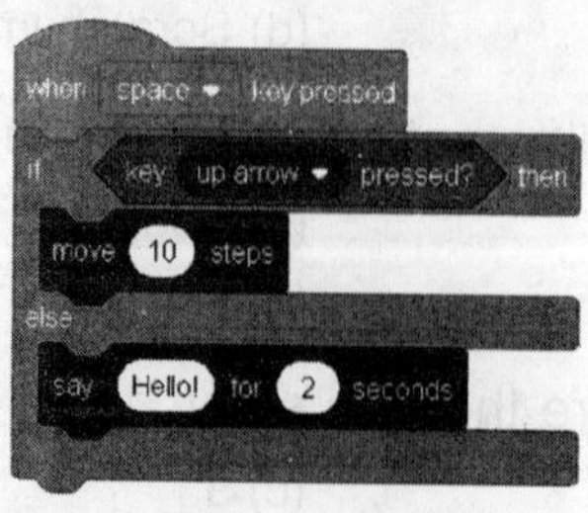

(a) Sprite will move 10 steps.
(b) Sprite will say hello for 2 seconds.
(c) Sprite will move 10 steps and say hello for 2 seconds.
(d) Nothing will happen.

18. What is the direction of the sprite shown in the image will be, when we click on the green flag from scratch window?

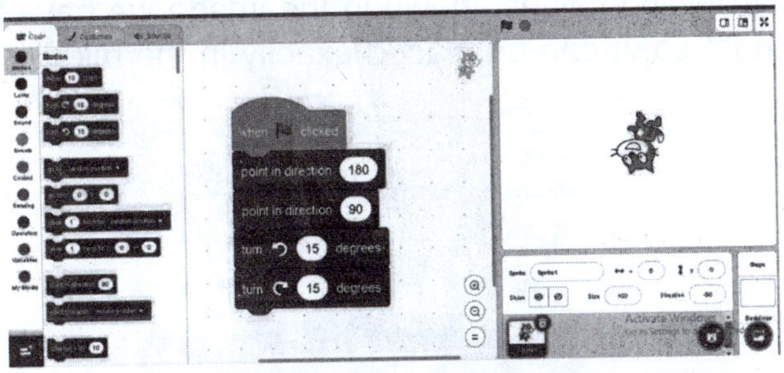

(a) 

(b) 

(c) 

(d) 

19. What is the outcome of the following code when user press space and enter 78?

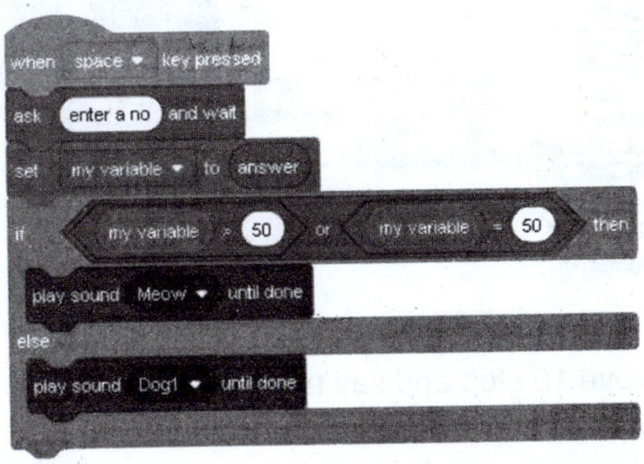

(a) Meow sound will play.
(b) Dog sound will play.
(c) Dog and meow sound will play.
(d) Nothing will happen.

MCQs 2 Marks Questions

20. Which of the following values shown in the image we have to change to move the sprite to right so, it can be placed exactly in the middle of the stage?

(a) ↕ y -90

(b) ↕ y -150

(c) Direction 0

(d) ↔ x 0

21. What will happen when you click on the marked icon on the image?

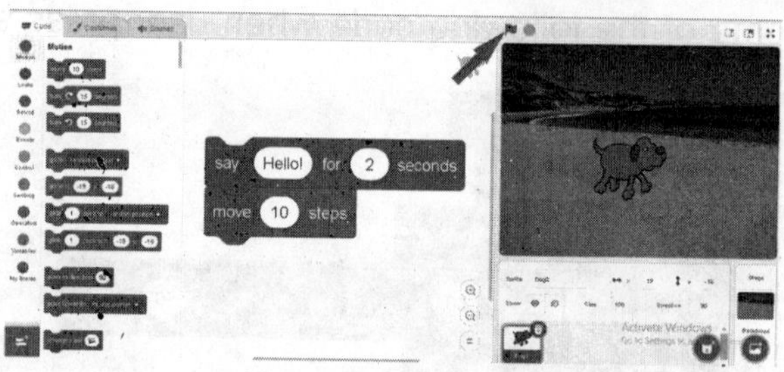

(a) The dog (sprite) move 10 steps and say hello.
(b) The dog (sprite) move 10 step and say hello for 2 sec.
(c) The dog (sprite) say hello for 2 sec and move 10 step.
(d) Nothing will happen.

22. Choose the incorrect statement about scratch.
(a) Scratch was developed by MIT media lab.
(b) Backdrop, sprite and blocks are assets for the scratch project.
(c) We can't add more than one sound to a sprite.
(d) We can't play multiple sounds at once.

23. Which of the following statements is/are correct about if () then, else block?

I. If the condition inside the if block is true than the blocks inside if will run.

II. In case of false condition the blocks inside else block will run.

III. If () then, else is a control script block's command block.

Codes

(a) Only I
(b) I and II
(c) Only III
(d) All of these

24. Choose the incorrect statement about variables in scratch.

(a) Global variable can be accessed or changed from any sprite in the stage.

(b) My variable is inbuilt variable in scratch.

(c) All sprites can use the local variable.

(d) We can use the variable to store names.

25. Match the script blocks with the number of blocks in it.

	List I		List II
A.	Motion	1.	8
B.	Control	2.	18
C.	Looks	3.	11
D.	Events	4.	20

Codes

	A	B	C	D
(a)	3	2	4	1
(b)	2	3	4	1
(c)	1	3	2	4
(d)	4	1	2	3

Darken your choice with HB Pencil

1.	(a) (b) (c) (d)	6.	(a) (b) (c) (d)	11.	(a) (b) (c) (d)	16.	(a) (b) (c) (d)	21.	(a) (b) (c) (d)
2.	(a) (b) (c) (d)	7.	(a) (b) (c) (d)	12.	(a) (b) (c) (d)	17.	(a) (b) (c) (d)	22.	(a) (b) (c) (d)
3.	(a) (b) (c) (d)	8.	(a) (b) (c) (d)	13.	(a) (b) (c) (d)	18.	(a) (b) (c) (d)	23.	(a) (b) (c) (d)
4.	(a) (b) (c) (d)	9.	(a) (b) (c) (d)	14.	(a) (b) (c) (d)	19.	(a) (b) (c) (d)	24.	(a) (b) (c) (d)
5.	(a) (b) (c) (d)	10.	(a) (b) (c) (d)	15.	(a) (b) (c) (d)	20.	(a) (b) (c) (d)	25.	(a) (b) (c) (d)

11

Internet and Its Uses

MCQs 1 Mark Questions

1. Internet is an example of
   (a) MAN (b) LAN (c) WAN (d) PAN
2. Internet service is first time started in India in 1995 by
   (a) BSNL (b) VSNL
   (c) Reliance (d) Vodafone
3. WWW is developed by
   (a) Brendan Eich (b) Tim Berners Lee
   (c) Weblink (d) Ada Lovelace
4. A text that is used to jump to other part of same page, or to load a new webpage is called
   (a) Hypertext (b) Hyperlink
   (c) Hotline (d) All of these
5. The address of a page/document on the www is known as
   (a) email address (b) URL
   (c) web address (d) Both (b) and (c)
6. Email was introduced by
   (a) Tim Berners Lee (b) Ray Tomlinson
   (c) William Gibson (d) Al Gore
7. A standard protocol that is used to send and receive email is
   (a) HTTP (b) SMTP (c) TCP/IP (d) ARP
8. A computer where server software is installed, which provides a variety of services to client software is known as
   (a) mail server (b) web server
   (c) proxy server (d) database server

9. A protocol which transmits IP address to domain name and vice versa.
(a) DNS (b) URL
(c) RARP (d) POP3

10. A type of website which indexes webpage on internet and provides information in the form of link is called
(a) web browser (b) web application
(c) search engine (d) web portal

11. A computer program which gather user's information through internet without their knowledge is called
(a) Antiware (b) Spyware
(c) Freeware (d) Shareware

12. A software application which is used to view, retrieve and send information on internet is known as
(a) web server (b) web browser
(c) search engine (d) block chain

13. .... is a freeware web browser which is developed by google.
(a) Chrome (b) Internet explorer
(c) Firefox (d) Opera

14. .... is a network model which is mainly developed for internet.
(a) OSI model (b) TCP/IP model
(c) Waterfall model (d) Spiral model

15. .... is the slowest internet connection service.
(a) Dialup service (b) TCP/IP connection
(c) Digital subscriber line (d) Landline

16. Unsent emails are stored in .... in an email system.
(a) Trash files (b) Draft folder
(c) Inbox folder (d) Unsent folder

17. The process of copying files from user computer to web computer is called
(a) downloading (b) uploading
(c) surfing (d) browsing

18. A process through which a person can access sensitive information from user computer in unauthorized manner is called
(a) stealing (b) spying
(c) hacking (d) hijacking

MCQs 2 Marks Questions

19. Which of the following statements is/are correct?
   I. Each computer connected to internet is mandated to have a unique IP address.
   II. Bing is a web search engine developed by Netscape.
   III. A website is a collection of interrelated webpages.

Codes

(a) I and II (b) Only I (c) I and III (d) Only III

20. Choose the incorrect statement about websites.
   (a) A website can contain single webpage or multiple webpages.
   (b) First page of a website is known as home page.
   (c) The information available on a dynamic website always remains same as sent to webserver.
   (d) Google, Facebook, Flipkart are examples of some publically accessible websites.

21. Which of the following statements is /are true?
   I. Webserver is known as phonebook of internet.
   II. A domain name is a unique and case sensitive human readable name which identifies a website on internet.
   III. A dialup connection is an access method that uses telephone line to connect with internet.

Codes

(a) Only II (b) II and III (c) I and II (d) All of these

22. Match the following lists.

List I	List II
A. http:/www.google.com	1. web browser
B. SMTP	2. URL
C. Microsoft edge	3. protocol

Codes

	A	B	C
(a)	3	1	2
(b)	1	2	3
(c)	2	3	1
(d)	1	3	2

Darken your choice with HB Pencil

1.	ⓐ ⓑ ⓒ ⓓ	5.	ⓐ ⓑ ⓒ ⓓ	9.	ⓐ ⓑ ⓒ ⓓ	13.	ⓐ ⓑ ⓒ ⓓ	17.	ⓐ ⓑ ⓒ ⓓ	21.	ⓐ ⓑ ⓒ ⓓ
2.	ⓐ ⓑ ⓒ ⓓ	6.	ⓐ ⓑ ⓒ ⓓ	10.	ⓐ ⓑ ⓒ ⓓ	14.	ⓐ ⓑ ⓒ ⓓ	18.	ⓐ ⓑ ⓒ ⓓ	22.	ⓐ ⓑ ⓒ ⓓ
3.	ⓐ ⓑ ⓒ ⓓ	7.	ⓐ ⓑ ⓒ ⓓ	11.	ⓐ ⓑ ⓒ ⓓ	15.	ⓐ ⓑ ⓒ ⓓ	19.	ⓐ ⓑ ⓒ ⓓ		
4.	ⓐ ⓑ ⓒ ⓓ	8.	ⓐ ⓑ ⓒ ⓓ	12.	ⓐ ⓑ ⓒ ⓓ	16.	ⓐ ⓑ ⓒ ⓓ	20.	ⓐ ⓑ ⓒ ⓓ		

12

Latest Developments in the Field of IT

MCQs 1 Mark Questions

1. Spam filters on email, songs recommendation on YouTube and drone robots are examples of
   (a) Cloud computing (b) Artificial Intelligence.
   (c) Robotics (d) None of these
2. .... is virtual assistant developed by apple.
   (a) Siri (b) Alexa
   (c) Cortana (d) Star helper
3. First company to provide 5G service in India.
   (a) Jio (b) Airtel
   (c) Vodafone (d) Aircel
4. AWS (Amazon Web Services) is related to
   (a) Communication network (b) Cloud computing
   (c) Internet of things (d) Artificial intelligence
5. A technology that used to perform high volume reputable tasks is
   (a) Robotic Process Automation
   (b) mechanical volume processing
   (c) Cloud computing
   (d) Cloud processing
6. Analyzing the day to day interactions of humans and converting it into data is called
   (a) datafication (b) conversion
   (c) data analytics (d) None of these

7. What is not a component of edge computing?
   (a) Internet of Things (b) Communication network
   (c) Cloud computing (d) Satellite devices

8. The blocks in blockchain are linked together using
   (a) encryption (b) cryptography
   (c) chain commands (d) data links

9. Which of the following is not related to blockchain?
   (a) Avalanche (b) Ethereum
   (c) IBM Block chain (d) Intel Block service

10. Technology that study's DNA is
   (a) Genomics (b) Bio science
   (c) Cryptography (d) None of these

11. Which of the following is not a payment system logo?
   (a) (b)
   (c) (d)

12. What is drop box?
   (a) Cloud storage service (b) 3D modeling device
   (c) Blockchain system (d) Electrical device

13. Which of the following is not an application of blockchain?
   (a) Money transfer (b) Internet of Things
   (c) Smart contract (d) Server manipulation

14. Qubit is related to
   (a) data science (b) quantum computing
   (c) edge computing (d) None of these

15. Google day dream is a
   (a) gamming application (b) virtual reality platform
   (c) text formatting (d) different shapes

16. MEMECH stands for
(a) Motion Estimation Motion Compensation
(b) Motion Emulator Motion Compensation
(c) Motion Encryption Motion Compression
(d) Motion Estimation Monotonic Compensation

MCQs 2 Marks Questions

17. Which of the following statements holds true about the given logo?

aws

I It is a cloud computing platform developed by AMAZON.
II. It provides payment services for seamless transactions.

Codes

(a) Only I (b) Only II
(c) Both I and II (d) Neither I nor II

18. Which of the following statement is/are true about Google home?
I. It is a cloud computing device developed by Google.
II. It is a software device for home security.

Codes

(a) Only I (b) Only II
(c) Both I and II (d) Neither I nor II

Darken your choice with HB Pencil

1.	ⓐ ⓑ ⓒ ⓓ	5.	ⓐ ⓑ ⓒ ⓓ	9.	ⓐ ⓑ ⓒ ⓓ	13.	ⓐ ⓑ ⓒ ⓓ	17.	ⓐ ⓑ ⓒ ⓓ
2.	ⓐ ⓑ ⓒ ⓓ	6.	ⓐ ⓑ ⓒ ⓓ	10.	ⓐ ⓑ ⓒ ⓓ	14.	ⓐ ⓑ ⓒ ⓓ	18.	ⓐ ⓑ ⓒ ⓓ
3.	ⓐ ⓑ ⓒ ⓓ	7.	ⓐ ⓑ ⓒ ⓓ	11.	ⓐ ⓑ ⓒ ⓓ	15.	ⓐ ⓑ ⓒ ⓓ		
4.	ⓐ ⓑ ⓒ ⓓ	8.	ⓐ ⓑ ⓒ ⓓ	12.	ⓐ ⓑ ⓒ ⓓ	16.	ⓐ ⓑ ⓒ ⓓ		

Practice Sets

1-3

Practice Set 01

Time : 60 Mins. Max. Marks : 60

General Instructions

1. This question paper contains 50 questions.
2. All questions are compulsory. There is no negative marking.
3. This question paper is divided into two parts; In Part I, there are 40 MCQs of 1 mark each while in Part II, there are 10 MCQs of 2 marks each.
4. Use HB pencil / Blue ball point pen to mark your choice of answer by darkening the circles on the OMR Sheet.

Part I

1. Electronic Numerical Integrator and Computer that uses electron tube that controls the flow of electrons in the vacuum, introduced in which computer generation?
   (a) Second generation (b) Third generation
   (c) Fourth generation (d) First generation
2. Magnetic core used in which generation of computer?
   (a) Third generation (b) Second generation
   (c) Fourth generation (d) None of these
3. Which one is not a type of computer code?
   (a) ASCII (b) BCD (c) EDIC (d) EBCDIC
4. Suppose your computer system is crashed and you restart the operating system what it is called?
   (a) Cold booting (b) Warm booting
   (c) Reloading (d) None of the above
5. Which of the following is not a system utility?
   (a) Antivirus (b) Volume control
   (c) Operating System (d) File management system
6. Michael uses application through a dialogue, recorded narration, music and sound effects. What kind of multimedia does he use?
   (a) animation (b) video (c) audio (d) radio
7. What does MPEG stand for?
   (a) Moving Pictures Enterprises Group (b) Moving Parts Excellence Group
   (c) Moving Picture Experts Group (d) Moving Picture Enterprise Group

8. What will you do to hide status Bar?

(a) Hide status bar from home tab
(b) uncheck status bar from view tab
(c) uncheck status bar from Home tab
(d) Click on hide status bar button

9. CTRL+E shortcut key is used in MS paint for

(a) draw an eclipse
(b) image properties
(c) center align
(d) menu

10. Which feature of MS Word allows us to include list of resources that used to write a document?

(a) reference (b) Bibliography (c) captions (d) citations

11. Google chrome book run on

(a) Google OS
(b) Chrome OS
(c) Android OS
(d) Chrome book OS

12. The supercomputer developed by Vijay Bhatkar is

(a) PARAM900
(b) PARAM8000
(c) ANURAG800
(d) SHAKTI8000

13. Windows enables various short cut keys that allow to perform a particular task quickly. Which one of the following key combinations is used to close the dialog box to close the current active window?

(a) Alt+F10 (b) Alt+F4 (c) Alt+F6 (d) Alt+F7

14. Uppercase on Change Case dialog box and All Caps on Fonts dialog box both converts selected text into Capital Letters. What's the difference between the two?

(a) Both are same. They are only two different ways of capitalize text.
(b) It is faster to convert from Change Case than from Font dialog box.
(c) Change Case makes conversion permanent but All Caps on Font can always be reverted.
(d) All Caps on Font dialog box makes the change permanent where Change Case can be always reverted.

15. The place where we type logo primitives is called

(a) main screen
(b) command input box
(c) console window
(d) command area

16. Word fields are inserted as .... in MS Word.

(a) Cross-reference
(b) Objects
(c) Placeholders
(d) Textbox

17. Which key is used to open help window in MS Word?

(a) F4 (b) F12 (c) F1 (d) F5

18. .... is a feature of MS Word which combines name and address with a standard document.
(a) Form letters (b) Mail merge
(c) Wrap text (d) Text formatting

19. Which one is not a master view option in Power Point?
(a) Outline master (b) Handout master
(c) Slide master (d) Notes master

20. Themes are available in which tab of MS Power Point?
(a) Insert tab (b) Home tab (c) Design tab (d) View tab

21. Which option automatically decreases the size of the font to fit in the place holder, while typing in place holder?
(a) Auto fit (b) Auto fit text to place holder
(c) Auto adjust (d) Text wrap

22. .... function of MS Excel is used to display row data in column or column data in a row.
(a) Transpose (b) Replace (c) vlookup (d) Transition

23. For comparing values we use .... in MS Excel.
(a) Line chart (b) Donut chart
(c) Pie chart (d) Column chart

24. Which of the following shortcut key is used to highlight the entire column in MS Excel.
(a) CTRL+H (b) CTRL+Space Bar
(c) CTRL+SHIFT+H (d) CTRL+F1

25. .... is used for network administration.
(a) SNMP (b) TFTP (c) DHCP (d) TELNET

26. The option that reduces the font size of the data to accommodate it within the column width is
(a) Shrink to fit (b) Columns
(c) Text orientation (d) Wrap text

27. What is the full form of IMAP-4?
(a) Internet Mailing Access Protocol 4th edition
(b) Internet Mail Access Protocol Version-4
(c) Internet Management and Administrative Protocol Version-4
(d) Internet Management Access Protocol 4

28. What is the full form of AIFF?

(a) Audio Interchange File Format
(b) Audio Incompetence File Formatting
(c) Automatic Interception File Format
(d) Automatic ASSCI File Format

29. Which shortcut key is used for view the picture in full screen in MS Paint?

(a) F12
(b) F1
(c) F11
(d) F6

30. By which option of control panel we can set themes?

(a) Personalization
(b) Themes
(c) Windows accessories
(d) Set themes

31. .... shows you the contents of your hard disk and floppy disk.

(a) Desktop
(b) My computer
(c) C drive
(d) Window

32. What is this part of computer?

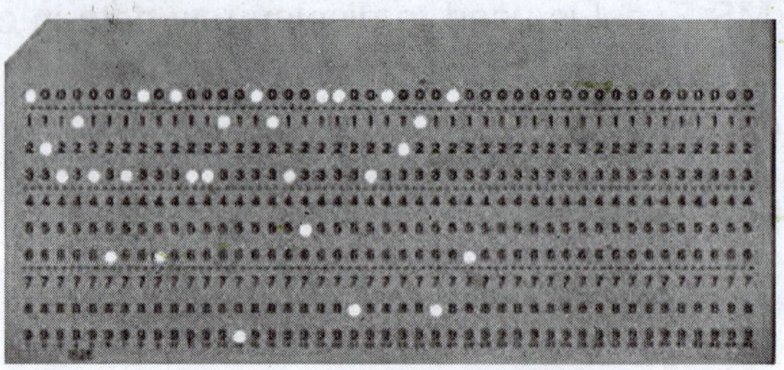

(a) CPU
(b) Punch card
(c) Keyboard
(d) Type writer

33. For keeping an observation on the website, the web browser stores the small text messages on the computer are called

(a) web service
(b) malware
(c) virus
(d) cookies

34. .org, .com, .gov, .net are the examples of

(a) websites
(b) host name
(c) domain name
(d) server domains

35. In the follc ving URL http://www.twitter.com, which part is the host name?

(a) http
(b) .com
(c) WWW
(d) Twitter

36. Which of the following block is used to end the script in scratch?

(a) END
(b) CAP
(c) DEL
(d) STOP

37. What will happen if you placed the instruction blocks in the wrong order in scratch?

(a) Nothing happens
(b) The program will not function properly
(c) The program will not run
(d) The program will run slow

38. Which type of music file is supported by scratch?

(a) MP3
(b) WAV
(c) MP4
(d) All of these

39. Which of the following app determines your global position by using GPS?

(a) Position navigator
(b) Trivago
(c) Mapptrix navigator
(d) Jubong

40. "PAi" is an Artificial Intelligence based Chatbot, launched by

(a) Security and Exchange Board of India
(b) National Payment Corporation of India
(c) Payment System Management of India
(d) National Payment Gateway of India

Part II

41. Which of the following statements is/are correct about analytical engine?

I. It is designed by Allen Turing in 1837.
II. It uses punch cards.
III. It is first general mechanical computer.

Codes

(a) Only I (b) Only II (c) II and III (d) All of these

42. Which of the following statements is/are correct about magnetic storage devices?

I. In magnetic storage devices data is stored using magnetize medium.
II. Magnetic storage devices are less expensive.
III. Zip diskette, floppy disk are some examples of magnetic storage devices.

Codes

(a) Only I (b) Only II (c) I and II (d) All of these

43. Match the following MS Word shortcut keys.

List I	List II
A. Ctrl+%	1. change the font
B. CTRL+H	2. center align
C. CTRL+E	3. line spacing to 1.5
D. CTRL+ SHIFT+F	4. find and replace

Codes

	A	B	C	D		A	B	C	D
(a)	2	3	1	4	(b)	4	2	3	1
(c)	3	4	2	1	(d)	4	3	2	1

44. Which one of the following statements holds true about MS PowerPoint?

I. Template is a file consist of readymade styles that we can use for our presentation.

II. You can insert text boxes from drawing toolbar in PowerPoint.

III. You can type text directly into a slide but typing in text box in more convenient.

Codes

(a) Only I
(b) Only II
(c) I and II
(d) All of these

45. Which of the following statements is/are incorrect about telnet?

I. It is used for remote login into a remote computer.

II. Telnet uses port number 23.

III. We can't access the files and resources of remote computer.

Codes

(a) Only I (b) Only II (c) Only III (d) II and III

46. Which one of the following statements is incorrect about LOGO?

(a) We can use the command right_180 to make the turtle take a half turn.

(b) Print [PR] primitive is used to display a character, number, word or sentence on the screen.

(c) The clean command is used to erase all lines in the graphics area and restores the turtle to its home position.

(d) The recall list box displays all the commands we have typed in the 'command input box'.

47. What will be the position of bat (sprite) is when we run the following code?

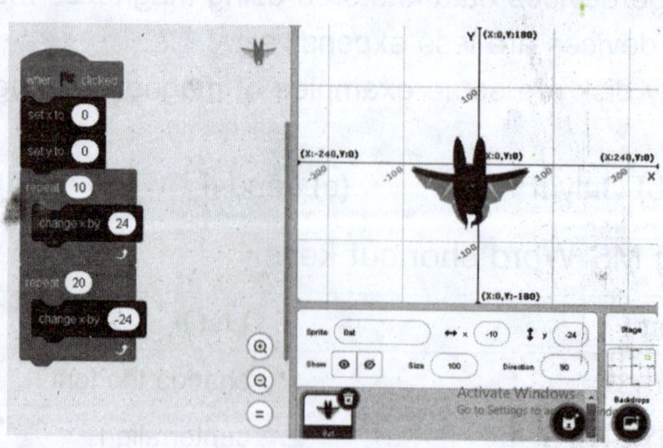

(a) x is -24 y is 24
(b) x is -240 y is -240
(c) x is -240 y is 0
(d) x is 0 y is 0

48. Which of the following statements is/are incorrect about IT?

I. While technology advancing in a rapid pace on industries and work, human workers still have much more value.

II. With advancement in the technology, communicating with people is become easier but also much more expensive.

III. It change the education system drastically, education system now adapted a modern way now a days gadgets have become important part of teaching method.

Codes

(a) Only I (b) I and II

(c) II and III (d) All of these

49. Select the incorrect statement about Windows 10.

(a) In windows 10 you cannot create multiple desktops.

(b) Window hello allows you to sign in your system data like finger print or face recognition.

(c) Windows media player is used to run and organize digital media file on a computer.

(d) Continuum allows you to change windows 10 into touch friendly interface.

50. Which of the following statement is/are true?

I. ISP is a company that gives you the access to the internet. The browser will not be able to display pages unless the computer is connected to an ISP.

II. To see any website on the internet you have to type its web address in the address bar of the web browser.

III. www.outlook.com, www.yahoo.com are some popular sites that provides the facility to send mails but we cannot receive mails from this websites.

Codes

(a) I and III (b) Only II

(c) I and II (d) All of these

Darken your choice with HB Pencil

1.	(a) (b) (c) (d)	10.	(a) (b) (c) (d)	19.	(a) (b) (c) (d)	28.	(a) (b) (c) (d)	37.	(a) (b) (c) (d)	46.	(a) (b) (c) (d)
2.	(a) (b) (c) (d)	11.	(a) (b) (c) (d)	20.	(a) (b) (c) (d)	29.	(a) (b) (c) (d)	38.	(a) (b) (c) (d)	47.	(a) (b) (c) (d)
3.	(a) (b) (c) (d)	12.	(a) (b) (c) (d)	21.	(a) (b) (c) (d)	30.	(a) (b) (c) (d)	39.	(a) (b) (c) (d)	48.	(a) (b) (c) (d)
4.	(a) (b) (c) (d)	13.	(a) (b) (c) (d)	22.	(a) (b) (c) (d)	31.	(a) (b) (c) (d)	40.	(a) (b) (c) (d)	49.	(a) (b) (c) (d)
5.	(a) (b) (c) (d)	14.	(a) (b) (c) (d)	23.	(a) (b) (c) (d)	32.	(a) (b) (c) (d)	41.	(a) (b) (c) (d)	50.	(a) (b) (c) (d)
6.	(a) (b) (c) (d)	15.	(a) (b) (c) (d)	24.	(a) (b) (c) (d)	33.	(a) (b) (c) (d)	42.	(a) (b) (c) (d)		
7.	(a) (b) (c) (d)	16.	(a) (b) (c) (d)	25.	(a) (b) (c) (d)	34.	(a) (b) (c) (d)	43.	(a) (b) (c) (d)		
8.	(a) (b) (c) (d)	17.	(a) (b) (c) (d)	26.	(a) (b) (c) (d)	35.	(a) (b) (c) (d)	44.	(a) (b) (c) (d)		
9.	(a) (b) (c) (d)	18.	(a) (b) (c) (d)	27.	(a) (b) (c) (d)	36.	(a) (b) (c) (d)	45.	(a) (b) (c) (d)		

Practice Set 02

Time : 60 Mins.

Max. Marks : 60

General Instructions

1. This question paper contains 50 questions.
2. All questions are compulsory. There is no negative marking.
3. This question paper is divided into two parts; In Part I, there are 40 MCQs of 1 mark each while in Part II, there are 10 MCQs of 2 marks each.
4. Use HB pencil / Blue ball point pen to mark your choice of answer by darkening the circles on the OMR Sheet.

Part I

1. Which one of the following is the first Microprocessor?
   (a) Intel 400
   (b) Intel 41
   (c) Intel 4004
   (d) Intel 4001

2. Paint 3D is replacement of ……… in Windows 10.
   (a) Paint HD
   (b) MS Paint
   (c) Paint 2D
   (d) All of the above

3. A Circuit board that works as a backbone of communications in computer and connects the different parts of computer together is known as
   (a) mainboard
   (b) backplane board
   (c) motherboard
   (d) All of the above

4. In which tab thumbnail option is available in paint?
   (a) Insert
   (b) Home
   (c) View
   (d) File

5. You can use the format painter in MS Excel multiple times before you turn it off by
   (a) You can use the format painter button only one time when you click it.
   (b) Double clicking the format painter button.
   (c) Pressing the Ctrl key and clicking the format painter button.
   (d) Pressing the Alt key and clicking the format painter button.

6. What is the active cell in MS Excel?
   (a) The bottom cell in a worksheet
   (b) The top cell in a worksheet
   (c) The Past cell in a worksheet
   (d) The current cell in a worksheet

7. It is a discussion or informational website published on the World Wide Web typically one run by an individual or small group, which is written in an informal or conversational style. What is it?
   (a) blog (b) vlog (c) webinars (d) video

8. Which of the following computer is used in weather forecasting?
   (a) Supercomputer (b) Micro computer
   (c) Mainframe computer (d) All of these

9. What manages and executes the boot sequence of a computer system?
   (a) CPU (b) Boot loader
   (c) Motherboard (d) Boot sequencer

10. EDSAC was first .... computer which is developed in .... of computers.
   (a) Full mechanical and programmable, Second generation
   (b) Full sized stored program, First generation
   (c) Fully scalable processing power, First generation
   (d) None of the above

11. Which of the following have the smallest file size for same image?
   (a) JPEG (b) PNG
   (c) SVG (d) All have same size

12. Which is the form of marketing that uses social media?
   (a) SMM (b) SNM (c) SMB (d) MFB

13. SVG use which format to define graphics?
   (a) Picture (b) Xml (c) Xhtml (d) Pixel

14. Apple smart watch is example of
   (a) Wearable technology (b) Watch technology
   (c) Wireless device (d) None of the above

15. Resizing an image is known as
   (a) designing (b) modification
   (c) manipulation (d) changing

16. Ctrl +F6 shortcut key is used for .... in MS Word.
   (a) help window (b) navigation panel
   (c) switch window (d) None of the above

17. Which one of the following tab we use to remove image background in MS Word?
   (a) Insert (b) Format (c) Home (d) Design

18. While writing a document what will you use to give credit to a source of information and from which tab of MS Word?
    (a) Table of authorities from references tab
    (b) Bibliography from review tab
    (c) Citations and bibliography from reference tab
    (d) Captions from references tab
19. In MS Excel, Pie chart is good when we have to deal with
    (a) number data (b) single series of data
    (c) image based data (d) None of the above
20. .... is used to create loop in scratch.
    (a) For (b) Repeat (c) Loop (d) If then
21. Which of the following can be used to eliminate unnecessary data and view only the data specified in a criteria?
    (a) Advanced view (b) Grid view (c) Filter (d) Sort
22. What is cell tip?
    (a) Comments put on cell (b) Information about cell based on some criteria
    (c) Cell filtering technique (d) Cell filling hint
23. .... allows you to quickly create your presentation by providing step by step guide.
    (a) Quick content (b) Auto content wizard
    (c) Content wizard (d) Quick content wizard
24. Which of the following allows you to quickly modify your slides and layout of your slides?
    (a) Outline view (b) Slide master
    (c) Slide editor (d) Slide sorter view
25. From which tab we can add audio and video in PowerPoint?
    (a) Media (b) Insert (c) Design (d) Animation
26. Disk defragmenter is a .... program in Microsoft windows.
    (a) software (b) system (c) application (d) utility
27. Which of the following is a disadvantage of in place upgrade in windows 10?
    (a) Slow down the computer system.
    (b) Creates pointless junk files and surplus registry entries.
    (c) Creates unnecessary trash files.
    (d) Chances of hard disk crashing increases.
28. From which setting we can change the display brightness in Windows 10?
    (a) Display (b) Personalization (c) Ease of Access (d) Both (a) and (c)

29. Which of the following is not a selection option in MS Paint?
(a) Rectangular selection form
(b) Grid selection
(c) Free form selection
(d) Invert selection

30. Modulation is the process of
(a) Sending a file from one computer to another computer
(b) Converting digital signals to analog signals
(c) Converting analog signals to digital signals
(d) Echoing every character that is received

31. Overloaded network nodes are related to
(a) network inefficiency
(b) network congestion
(c) network collision
(d) network overloading

32. What is the name of the device that connects two computers by means of a telephone line?
(a) Tape (b) Modem (c) Bus (d) Cable

33. Which of the following network device uses multiple communication protocol?
(a) Bridge (b) Router (c) Gateway (d) Brouter

34. .... is a model of a set of problems or events that can be used to teach someone how to do something, or the process of making such a model.
(a) Website (b) Simulation (c) Game (d) Print media

35. Which of the following refers to alternate appearances of a sprite in scratch?
(a) Costume
(b) Change appearance
(c) Change book
(d) Output

36. The word wrap feature
(a) Automatically move text to the next line when necessary
(b) Appears at the bottom of the document
(c) Allows you to type over text
(d) Is the short horizontal line

37. .... is used to establish wireless communication between two devices and provide a secure way for transactions and other data sharing activities.
(a) NFC (b) NIC (c) NPC (d) NCF

38. Auto clipart is a feature that
(a) Automatically places clipart in your presentation
(b) Scans your presentation for incorrect spelling in your words on each slide
(c) Scans your presentation for incorrect spelling in Word Arts objects
(d) All of the above

39. Laptop launched by Google

(a) Chrome home processor (b) Google pixel book

(c) Chrome book (d) Google nexus book

40. What will be the output of the following code when we press space ?

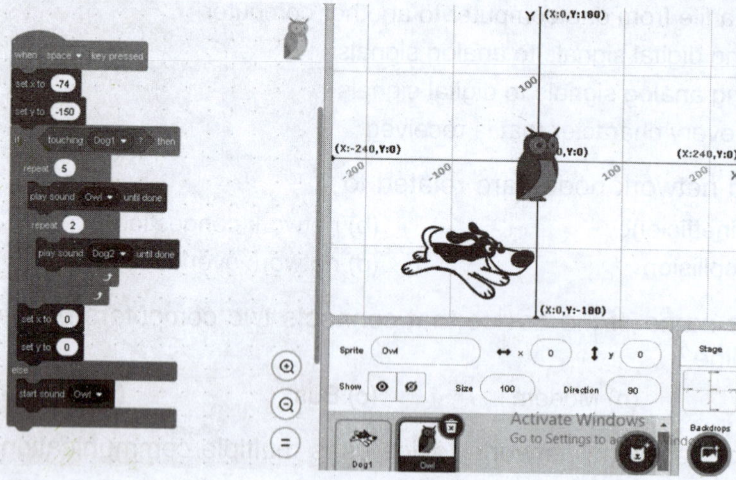

(a) Owl sound plays five times and then dog sound plays two times and position of owl is right end.

(b) Owl sound plays once and then dog sound will play for two times and this continues for four more times than owl goes to the center of the stage.

(c) Owl sound plays and then dog sound will play for ten times.

(d) Owl sound plays five times then dog sound will play for two times and this continues for four more times than owl goes to the center of the stage.

Part II

41. Which of the following is/are correct statements about generation of computers?

I. IC were used in fourth generation of computers.

II. pdp-8 is popular computer of third generation.

III. Intel 4004 chip is developed in fourth generation of computers.

Codes

(a) Only I (b) Only II (c) Only III (d) All of these

42. Which of the following statements is/are correct about RAM?

I. RAM is a non-volatile memory.

II. In RAM data can be modify in any order.

III. DRAM is faster in comparison of SRAM.

Codes

(a) Only I (b) Only II (c) I and II (d) All of these

43. Which of the following is not a valid advantage of multimedia?

I. Multimedia doesn't required significant investment.

II. Multimedia provides greater flexibility.

III. Multimedia doesn't depends on the marketing for success.

Codes

(a) Only I
(b) I and II
(c) I and II
(d) All of these

44. Match the following lists.

	List I		List II
A.	Line chart	1.	Show Single data series
B.	Bar chart	2.	Show Change over time
C.	Scatter chart	3.	Show quantitative data
D.	Area chart	4.	Show and compare numeric values

Codes

	A	B	C	D
(a)	2	1	4	3
(b)	3	4	1	2
(c)	1	2	4	3
(d)	4	3	1	2

45. Choose the correct steps to create custom slide show in PowerPoint.

(a) Click on slide show tab->under setup slide show click add custom slides->click custom shows->click new->select slides to add->click on add.

(b) Click on slide show tab->under start slide show click custom slide show->click custom slides->select slides to add.

(c) Click on slide show tab->under setup click present slide show->click custom shows->select slides to add->click on add.

(d) Click on slide show tab->under start slide show click custom slide show->click custom shows->click new->select slides to add->click on add.

46. Choose the incorrect statement about Google drive.

(a) Google drive is developed and launched by Google in 2012.

(b) Google drive is cloud storage service.

(c) Google drive provides 15 gigabyte of free space.

(d) None of the above

47. Choose the wrong statement about hub.

(a) Hub is mainly used in LAN.

(b) Active hub works as a repeater.

(c) Hub is useful for configuring LAN with star topology.

(d) Passive hub provides signal regeneration facility.

48. Match the following lists.

List I	List II
A. AI	1. Sumo logic
B. IoT	2. Amazon web services
C. Robotics	3. Azure
D. Data science	4. Aethon

Codes

	A	B	C	D
(a)	3	1	2	4
(b)	2	3	4	1
(c)	3	1	4	2
(d)	1	3	4	2

49. Which of the following statement is correct?

I. Microsoft Cortana in Windows 10 can recognize natural voices without any input of keyboard.

II. It allows users to set reminders based on location and time.

Codes

(a) Only I
(b) Only II
(c) Both I and II
(d) Neither I nor II

50. Choose the correct statements about Windows 10.

I. Copying music, images and videos from a CD to computer is called ripping.

II. To change the appearance of the desktop, windows we can apply themes on a computer form the control panel.

III. We use the shortcut key CTRL+S to stop currently playing song in the windows media player.

Codes

(a) I and II
(b) Only II
(c) I and II
(d) All of these

Darken your choice with HB Pencil

1. ⓐ ⓑ ⓒ ⓓ	10. ⓐ ⓑ ⓒ ⓓ	19. ⓐ ⓑ ⓒ ⓓ	28. ⓐ ⓑ ⓒ ⓓ	37. ⓐ ⓑ ⓒ ⓓ	46. ⓐ ⓑ ⓒ ⓓ
2. ⓐ ⓑ ⓒ ⓓ	11. ⓐ ⓑ ⓒ ⓓ	20. ⓐ ⓑ ⓒ ⓓ	29. ⓐ ⓑ ⓒ ⓓ	38. ⓐ ⓑ ⓒ ⓓ	47. ⓐ ⓑ ⓒ ⓓ
3. ⓐ ⓑ ⓒ ⓓ	12. ⓐ ⓑ ⓒ ⓓ	21. ⓐ ⓑ ⓒ ⓓ	30. ⓐ ⓑ ⓒ ⓓ	39. ⓐ ⓑ ⓒ ⓓ	48. ⓐ ⓑ ⓒ ⓓ
4. ⓐ ⓑ ⓒ ⓓ	13. ⓐ ⓑ ⓒ ⓓ	22. ⓐ ⓑ ⓒ ⓓ	31. ⓐ ⓑ ⓒ ⓓ	40. ⓐ ⓑ ⓒ ⓓ	49. ⓐ ⓑ ⓒ ⓓ
5. ⓐ ⓑ ⓒ ⓓ	14. ⓐ ⓑ ⓒ ⓓ	23. ⓐ ⓑ ⓒ ⓓ	32. ⓐ ⓑ ⓒ ⓓ	41. ⓐ ⓑ ⓒ ⓓ	50. ⓐ ⓑ ⓒ ⓓ
6. ⓐ ⓑ ⓒ ⓓ	15. ⓐ ⓑ ⓒ ⓓ	24. ⓐ ⓑ ⓒ ⓓ	33. ⓐ ⓑ ⓒ ⓓ	42. ⓐ ⓑ ⓒ ⓓ	
7. ⓐ ⓑ ⓒ ⓓ	16. ⓐ ⓑ ⓒ ⓓ	25. ⓐ ⓑ ⓒ ⓓ	34. ⓐ ⓑ ⓒ ⓓ	43. ⓐ ⓑ ⓒ ⓓ	
8. ⓐ ⓑ ⓒ ⓓ	17. ⓐ ⓑ ⓒ ⓓ	26. ⓐ ⓑ ⓒ ⓓ	35. ⓐ ⓑ ⓒ ⓓ	44. ⓐ ⓑ ⓒ ⓓ	
9. ⓐ ⓑ ⓒ ⓓ	18. ⓐ ⓑ ⓒ ⓓ	27. ⓐ ⓑ ⓒ ⓓ	36. ⓐ ⓑ ⓒ ⓓ	45. ⓐ ⓑ ⓒ ⓓ	

Practice Set 03

Time : 60 Mins. Max. Marks : 60

General Instructions

1. This question paper contains 50 questions.
2. All questions are compulsory. There is no negative marking.
3. This question paper is divided into two parts; In Part I, there are 40 MCQs of 1 mark each while in Part II, there are 10 MCQs of 2 marks each.
4. Use HB pencil / Blue ball point pen to mark your choice of answer by darkening the circles on the OMR Sheet.

Part I

1. Which of the following is a Second generation computer?

(a) EDVAC (b) ENIAC
(c) UNIVAC 1108 (d) All of these

2. What is the correct cycle of data processing?

(a) Input-processing-storage-output (b) Input-storage-processing-output
(c) Input-processing-output-storage (d) None of these

3. Which of the following is an input device?

(a) Paddle (b) Wi-Fi remote
(c) Digital camera (d) All of these

4. Logical error in a computer is known as

(a) virus (b) bug
(c) error (d) fault

5. Audacity is a

(a) audio editing and recording application.
(b) video rendering and editing application.
(c) graphic designing and publishing website.
(d) multimedia managing and creating application.

6. What is the full form of SVG?

(a) Scalable Vented Graphics (b) Scalable Vector Graphics
(c) Sustainable Vector Graphics (d) Scalable Verity Graphics

7. Scratch is developed by

(a) Dennis Ritchi
(b) Mitchel Resnick
(c) Tom Harold
(d) Tim Berners Lee

8. A person can understand the content regardless of the location, which advantage of multimedia is this?

(a) Highly flexible
(b) Communication freedom
(c) Better personal communication
(d) Location flexibility

9. Which one is not a brush in MS Paint?

(a) Water color brush
(b) Crayon
(c) Calligraphy brush
(d) None of the above

10. Ruler option is available in which tab of MS Paint?

(a) View
(b) Design
(c) Home
(d) Review

11. Shortcut key to open the resize and skew dialog box in MS Paint.

(a) CTRL+E
(b) CTRL+W
(c) CTRL+T
(d) CTRL+R

12. The blank space outside the printing area on a page is called ……… in a word document.

(a) margins
(b) header area
(c) free space
(d) alignment

13. How many types of tab stops are there in MS Word?

(a) 3
(b) 4
(c) 5
(d) 2

14. Choose the correct steps to change a page number style from A, B, C……to a,b,c…. in MS Word document.

(a) Insert tab-> header and footer-> page number-> format page number
(b) Design tab-> heading tab->text page number->format page
(c) Insert tab-> header > page number-> format page number
(d) Format-> header and footer-> format page number

15. Which tool is used to spray colors in MS Paint ?

(a) Fill color
(b) Airbrush
(c) brush
(d) Calibri brush

16. Coaxial cable is a type of

(a) unbounded media
(b) wireless casting
(c) bounded media
(d) None of these

17. THINNET is a

(a) cable medium
(b) wireless transmission
(c) type of terminals
(d) network based transmission tool

18. Twisted pair cables are used in

(a) Medium distance communication
(b) Long distance communication
(c) Short distance communication.
(d) Both (a) and (c)

19. What is the output of the question when we press space and enter Rohit as first name and Kumawat as last name?

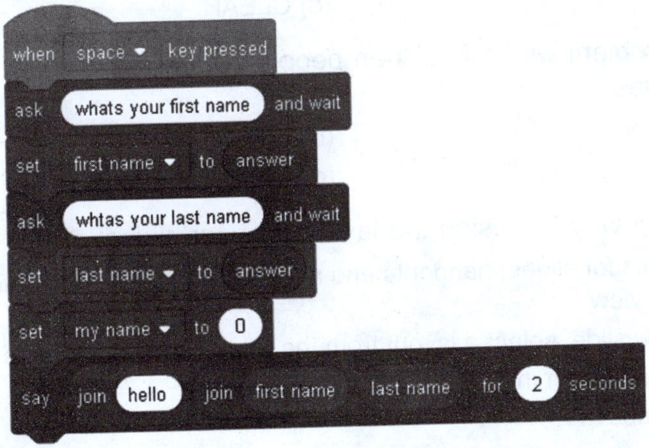

(a) Rohit Kumawat
(b) Hellow Rohit Kumawat
(c) Hello first name last name
(d) Hello Rohit Kumawat

20. Which option is used to move something in very specific way on a slide?

(a) Animation effect
(b) Transitions
(c) Motion path
(d) Slide animation

21. .... command is used in PowerPoint to change the color of different objects without changing content.

(a) Color scheme
(b) Clipart
(c) Design template
(d) Adjust color

22. Which one is not a part of task pane?

(a) Slide layout
(b) Master slide
(c) Search results
(d) Clip art

23. For enter current date and time in a cell we use .... function in MS Excel.

(a) =TIME()
(b) =CURRENTTIME()
(c) =TODAYDATE( )
(d) =NOW()

24. Conditional formatting option is available in which group of home tab in Excel.
(a) Styles group
(b) Editing group
(c) Formula group
(d) Mailing group

25. The first version of MS Excel is released in
(a) 2000
(b) 1985
(c) 1991
(d) 1999

26. Which primitive clears the main screen in logo but does not send the turtle back to its home. It stays wherever it was.
(a) CLEARSCREEN
(b) CLEAN
(c) CLEARTEXT
(d) CLEAR

27. If there is a problem with the ... then people on the network will be unable to access their files.
(a) Internet server
(b) File server
(c) Mail server
(d) Database server

28. What's the best way to design the layout for your slides?
(a) Create layouts for slides, handouts and notes using the Master Layout dialog box in slide master view
(b) For each new slide, select a layout from the Slide Layout task pane
(c) Apply templates from the Slide Design task pane
(d) None of the above

29. CTRL, SHIFT and ALT keys on keyboard are known as
(a) function
(b) alternation
(c) modifiers
(d) control keys

30. In memory management, CPU fetch instructions on the basis of …… memory value.
(a) Memory address register
(b) Program counter register
(c) Cache
(d) Random access memory

31. To provide information on locating local stores that sales essential products "nearby spot" is an excellent initiative. Which firm started the initiative?
(a) Google
(b) Flipkart
(c) Microsoft
(d) Samsung

32. ……… removes the unnecessary files form your hard disk to run faster.
(a) Antivirus
(b) Disk clean up
(c) Disk fragmentary
(d) Clean up wizard

33. Windows has many utility programs for day to day applications which are known as
(a) applications
(b) utility
(c) accessories
(d) function software's

34. The area which shows temporary icons is called
(a) Notification area (b) Task panel
(c) desktop (d) This pc

35. .... is a free of cost repair of software bug available at internet.
(a) Anti bug (b) Antivirus
(c) Patch (d) Malware patcher

36. Verifying login name and password is known as
(a) configuration (b) login
(c) authentication (d) security check

37. A frequently updated online personal journal or diary is known as
(a) journal (b) encyclopedia (c) news group (d) blog

38. A new feature called 'fleets' is launched by which social media platform in India?
(a) Twitter (b) Instagram (c) Whatsapp (d) Skype

39. An AI (Artificial Intelligence) system to read algebra word problems and solve them is known as
(a) Math solver (b) Alexa (c) Backon (d) Stud

40. Sprites and scripts are stored in .... in a scratch screen.
(a) blocks palette (b) backpack
(c) stage (d) background

Part II

41. Choose the correct statements about computer generations.
I. First generation computer are very large and take a full room to fit.
II. Second generation of computer was from 1960 to 1967 and uses transistors.
III. Assembly language was used in first generation of computers.
IV. First microprocessor was used in 1971.

Codes
(a) I and II (b) I and III (c) I and IV (d) All of these

42. Choose the correct statements about MS Word.
I. The replace command allows you to find a word in document and replace it with another word.
II. You can select a sentence by holding down the shift key and clicking anywhere on the sentence.
III. The quick access toolbar of MS word consist buttons which are used to access the commonly used commands.

Codes

(a) I and II
(b) I and III
(c) Only III
(d) All of these

43. Which of the following statements is/are not true?

I. TCP is a connectionless protocol whereas UDP is a connection based protocol.
II. TCP provides acknowledgment that packet is received but UDP doesn't have acknowledgment segment.
III. TCP supports broadcasting whereas UDP doesn't supports broadcasting.

Codes

(a) I and II
(b) I and III
(c) Only II
(d) All of these

44. Which of the following statement is not true about MS PowerPoint?

(a) You can show and hide task pane form view-> toolbars.
(b) You cannot delete the objects in the premade slides layout.
(c) You can view a PowerPoint presentation in normal slide sorter or slide show view.
(d) When we delete a text box object from a slide in PowerPoint presentation, both textbox and text are deleted.

45. Which of the following statement is not true about computer memory?

(a) Computer memory holds data in electronic form and access the data only in random fashion.
(b) RAM, ROM and cache is example of computer memory.
(c) Cache and RAM are volatile memory.
(d) EPROM is used for debugging.

46. Choose the correct statement about multimedia.

I. Linear multimedia is used in workshops and seminars.
II. Multimedia can be used to provide education in interactive way.
III. 2d 3d animation is part of multimedia.

Codes

(a) I and II
(b) I and III
(c) Only II
(d) All of these

47. Which of the following is not an advantage of MS Excel?

I. Excel is best for financial and accounting work.
II. MS Excel is simple and easy to learn.
III. We can easily detect errors from millions of records in excel.

Codes

(a) Only I
(b) Only II
(c) II and III
(d) All of these

48. Match the following lists.

List I	List II
A. F11	1. show or hide the ruler
B. CTRL+G	2. show the context menu
C. CTRL+R	3. view picture in full screen mode
D. SHIFT+F10	4. show/hide gridline view

Codes

	A	B	C	D
(a)	3	1	4	2
(b)	1	2	3	4
(c)	4	3	1	2
(d)	3	4	1	2

49. Observe the following steps of MS Windows?

Start → All Programs → ? → Snipping Tool

Which of the following options will replace the question mark(?).

(a) System Tools
(b) Games
(c) Accessories
(d) Pictures

50. What is true about W3C?

I. It creates and publish web standards.
II. Development of web is dependent on W3C.
III. It is founded on 2001 by Tim Berners lee.

Codes

(a) Only I
(b) Only II
(c) I and II
(d) II and III

Darken your choice with HB Pencil

1.	a b c d	10.	a b c d	19.	a b c d	28.	a b c d	37.	a b c d	46.	a b c d
2.	a b c d	11.	a b c d	20.	a b c d	29.	a b c d	38.	a b c d	47.	a b c d
3.	a b c d	12.	a b c d	21.	a b c d	30.	a b c d	39.	a b c d	48.	a b c d
4.	a b c d	13.	a b c d	22.	a b c d	31.	a b c d	40.	a b c d	49.	a b c d
5.	a b c d	14.	a b c d	23.	a b c d	32.	a b c d	41.	a b c d	50.	a b c d
6.	a b c d	15.	a b c d	24.	a b c d	33.	a b c d	42.	a b c d		
7.	a b c d	16.	a b c d	25.	a b c d	34.	a b c d	43.	a b c d		
8.	a b c d	17.	a b c d	26.	a b c d	35.	a b c d	44.	a b c d		
9.	a b c d	18.	a b c d	27.	a b c d	36.	a b c d	45.	a b c d		

Answers *and* Explanations

Chapter 1

1. (b) **2.** (a) **3.** (c) **4.** (a) **5.** (b) **6.** (a) **7.** (b) **8.** (a) **9.** (a) **10.** (a)
11. (c) **12.** (c) **13.** (c) **14.** (c) **15.** (b) **16.** (d) **17.** (b) **18.** (c) **19.** (d) **20.** (d)
21. (b) **22.** (a) **23.** (a) **24.** (a) **25.** (a)

26. (a) ENIAC was designed by John Mauchly and J. Presper Eckert.

Chapter 2

1. (c) **2.** (a) **3.** (b) **4.** (a) **5.** (a) **6.** (c) **7.** (a) **8.** (b) **9.** (b) **10.** (d)
11. (c) **12.** (b) **13.** (a) **14.** (b) **15.** (b) **16.** (b)

17. (b) The program and data is located before ALU and Control Unit of a computer in internal memory, not in secondary memory or in disk.

18. (a) **19.** (a) The word is SOFTWARE.

20. (b) The main directory of a disk is called ROOT.

21. (c) **22.** (a)

Chapter 3

1. (c) **2.** (a) **3.** (b) **4.** (d) **5.** (d) **6.** (a) **7.** (c) **8.** (a)

9. (b) A file extension tells its type. Multimedia files commonly have .png, .wav, .mp3, .mpeg extensions.

10. (c) **11.** (a) **12.** (a) **13.** (c) **14.** (b) **15.** (d) **16.** (a) **17.** (b) **18.** (a)

19. (b) .WAV file format is supported by many browsers and doesn't need any plug in.

20. (c)

Chapter 4

1. (b) **2.** (d) **3.** (c)

4. (a) .bmp is bit map image file is a raster graphics image file format used to store bitmap digital images, independently of the display device.

5. (b) **6.** (d) **7.** (d) **8.** (d) **9.** (b) **10.** (c)
11. (c) **12.** (b) **13.** (a) **14.** (a) **15.** (c) **16.** (d) **17.** (a) **18.** (a) **19.** (a) **20.** (d)
21. (a) **22.** (a) **23.** (c)

24. (a) In the picture given in question, you can view image details in the following order, Cursor position, Selection size, Image size.

25. (c) This type of Stroke can be made by using Marker option in brushes tool.

26. (a)

27. (a) Maximum size to which you magnify the picture is 8X.

Chapter 5

1. (a) **2.** (c)

3. (d) Superscript is letter or number that is written above the normal line of type. AB is an example of superscript where number 2 is superscripted (written above the baseline).

4. (a) **5.** (b) **6.** (a) **7.** (a)

8. (b) Hyperlink is a clickable icon, graphic or text that links to another file or document. By clicking on hyperlink we can directly jump to another part of document or any other resource.

9. (d) **10.** (a) **11.** (b) **12.** (b) **13.** (a) **14.** (b) **15.** (a) **16.** (a)

17. (a) Drop cap feature is available in insert tab of MS Word. It is used to make first letter of a paragraph capital and larger than the remaining text. Drop cap is used as a decorative element in document.

18. (c) **19.** (a) **20.** (c) **21.** (c) **22.** (c) **23.** (b) **24.** (a) **25.** (c)

Chapter 6

1. (b) **2.** (c) **3.** (b) **4.** (c) **5.** (b) **6.** (b) **7.** (b) **8.** (a)

9. (b) CONCATENATE is a text function of MS Excel which helps to join two or more strings into a single string.

10. (b) **11.** (a)

12. (a) The freeze pane option of MS excel allows us to lock columns and rows so that when we scroll to view rest of the sheet, the rows and columns that are frozen will remain on the screen. We can use the freeze pane function from the view tab.

13. (c) **14.** (b) **15.** (d) **16.** (d) **17.** (b) **18.** (c)

19. (c) Process of changing the values of cells on a worksheet and analyzing how the changes affect the formulas in worksheet is called what if analysis.

20. (c) **21.** (b) **22.** (d) **23.** (b) **24.** (b) **25.** (c) **26.** (c) **27.** (c)

Chapter 7

1. (a) **2.** (c) **3.** (b) **4.** (b) **5.** (a)

6. (c) Template is the feature of MS PowerPoint which creates a sample slide show containing various layouts and themes.

7. (c) **8.** (a) **9.** (a)

10. (c) In slide sorter view we can change the order of slides, delete and insert new slides, add different transitions and set the timing for the slide show. It displays a miniature view of all the slides in a presentation.

11. (d) **12.** (b) **13.** (b) **14.** (c) **15.** (c) **16.** (c) **17.** (b) **18.** (b) **19.** (b) **20.** (b)

21. (c) **22.** (c) **23.** (a) **24.** (a) **25.** (b) **26.** (d) **27.** (a)

Chapter 8

1. (c) **2.** (a) **3.** (a) **4.** (c) **5.** (d) **6.** (c) **7.** (c) **8.** (a) **9.** (b) **10.** (c)

11. (b) **12.** (b) **13.** (c) **14.** (c) **15.** (c) **16.** (c) **17.** (c) **18.** (d) **19.** (b) **20.** (c)

21. (c) 22. (d) 23. (b)

Chapter 9

1. (d)
2. (b) PAN (Private Area Network) is a type of network which is mainly used by a user to connect their personal devices. Bluetooth is an example of private area network.
3. (b) ARPANET (Advance Research Project Agency Network) is a first Wide Area Network (WAN) which is developed by ARPA in 1969. ARPANET is based on TCP/IP network model.
4. (d)
5. (b) Terminals that does not require any external server for data processing is called thick client and the terminal that depend fully on an external server for processing and only display the data processed on server is called thin client.
   Hybrid client is a mixture of thin and thick client in which data processing is done locally but it depends on a server for data storage.

6. (d) 7. (c) 8. (b)

9. (b) Protocol is a set of rules and regulations which are used to provide variety of services on network and define communication.

10. (c) 11. (d) 12. (d)
13. (a) 14. (a) 15. (b) 16. (b) 17. (b) 18. (c) 19. (a) 20. (d)

21. (c) Bridge is a network device which is used to regenerate signals but cannot convert protocols. It is mainly used to separate network traffic.

22. (c) 23. (c) 24. (b)

Chapter 10

1. (c) 2. (c) 3. (b) 4. (b) 5. (c) 6. (a) 7. (c) 8. (d) 9. (b) 10. (b)
11. (c) 12. (b) 13. (b) 14. (d) 15. (a) 16. (b) 17. (b) 18. (d) 19. (a) 20. (d)
21. (d) 22. (c) 23. (d) 24. (c) 25. (b)

Chapter 11

1. (c) 2. (b) 3. (b) 4. (b) 5. (d) 6. (b) 7. (b) 8. (b) 9. (a) 10. (c)
11. (b) 12. (b) 13. (a) 14. (b) 15. (a) 16. (b) 17. (b) 18. (c) 19. (c) 20. (c)
21. (b) 22. (c)

Chapter 12

1. (b) 2. (a) 3. (b) 4. (b) 5. (a) 6. (a) 7. (d) 8. (b) 9. (d) 10. (a)
11. (c) 12. (a) 13. (d) 14. (b) 15. (b)

16. (a) MEMECH is stands for Motion Estimation Motion Compensation. MEMECH is used to improve the frame rate of video and make it smoother.

17. (a) 18. (d)

Practice Set 1

1. (d)	2. (b)	3. (c)	4. (b)	5. (c)	6. (c)	7. (c)	8. (b)	9. (b)	10. (b)
11. (b)	12. (b)	13. (b)	14. (c)	15. (b)	16. (a)	17. (c)	18. (b)	19. (a)	20. (c)
21. (b)	22. (a)	23. (d)	24. (b)	25. (a)	26. (a)	27. (b)	28. (a)	29. (c)	30. (a)
31. (b)	32. (b)	33. (d)	34. (c)	35. (d)	36. (b)	37. (b)	38. (d)	39. (c)	40. (b)
41. (c)	42. (d)	43. (c)	44. (c)	45. (c)	46. (c)	47. (c)	48. (b)	49. (a)	50. (c)

Practice Set 2

1. (c)	2. (b)	3. (d)	4. (c)	5. (b)	6. (d)	7. (a)	8. (a)	9. (b)	10. (b)
11. (a)	12. (a)	13. (b)	14. (a)	15. (b)	16. (c)	17. (b)	18. (c)	19. (b)	20. (b)
21. (c)	22. (a)	23. (b)	24. (b)	25. (b)	26. (d)	27. (b)	28. (d)	29. (b)	30. (b)
31. (b)	32. (b)	33. (c)	34. (b)	35. (a)	36. (a)	37. (a)	38. (d)	39. (b)	40. (b)
41. (d)	42. (b)	43. (b)	44. (a)	45. (d)	46. (d)	47. (d)	48. (b)	49. (c)	50. (d)

Practice Set 3

1. (c)	2. (a)	3. (d)	4. (b)	5. (a)	6. (b)	7. (b)	8. (a)	9. (d)	10. (a)
11. (b)	12. (a)	13. (b)	14. (a)	15. (b)	16. (c)	17. (a)	18. (d)	19. (d)	20. (c)
21. (a)	22. (b)	23. (d)	24. (a)	25. (b)	26. (b)	27. (b)	28. (b)	29. (c)	30. (b)
31. (a)	32. (b)	33. (c)	34. (a)	35. (c)	36. (c)	37. (d)	38. (a)	39. (a)	40. (b)
41. (c)	42. (b)	43. (b)	44. (b)	45. (a)	46. (d)	47. (c)	48. (d)	49. (c)	50. (c)